E-mailing Chris that day was one of the best decisions I've made in my professional life. He was not only interested in the ideas I had to share with him about how to make his story better for readers, he was willing to get to work immediately to make those changes happen. In a very short period of time, Chris came back to me with a version of Chickenhare that felt like it belonged on my bookshelf next to Bone and Usagi Yojimbo and Little Lulu. Chris had taken the smallest amount of encouragement and direction and—with his incredible vision, creativity, and drive—turned his rough idea into a fully realized adventure story that felt like an instant classic. And I wasn't the only one who thought so—mere months after his first-ever book was released, Chris was nominated for an Eisner Award in the category of Best Title for a Younger Audience for his work on Chickenhare.

That's the alchemy I mentioned above—creative brains working together to make the very best version of a story come to life. And in this case, I was doubly lucky. In meeting Chris and working with him to develop Chickenhare, I not only found a great new talent to bring into the world of comics, I found a great friend, too—someone I hope I get to work with for the rest of my career.

All of this Chickenhare origin story stuff happened many years ago at this point, but I still talk to Chris on an almost daily basis, and we are still mashing our weird brains together to make his incredible, far-flung ideas into books that will be read for generations to come. I know that I feel lucky to have stumbled upon the weird magic that emanates from Chris's incredible talent and creativity, and I hope you feel the same after you spend some time with Chickenhare and his friends.

Shawna Gore
Portland, Oregon

CHICKENHARE

THE HOUSE OF KLAUS

WRITTEN & ILLUSTRATED BY
CHRIS GRINE

DESIGN BY
MICHAEL DEVITO

EDITING BY
DAVID A. RODRIGUEZ

3WS
WWW.TH3RDWORLD.COM

PUBLISHER
MICHAEL DEVITO

BUSINESS DIRECTOR
KENNY WELKER

To the fans who even after sixteen
years still want more Chickenhare.
You're crazy, but I love you all.

-Chris

COME ON, BARLEY. YOU DON'T REALLY WANT TO SELL US TO THIS WEIRD COLLECTOR GUY, ***RIGHT?***
OH ***YES***, I DO!
AND SHUT YER ***DANG*** MOUTHS. I TOLD YA ALREADY WE DON'T WANT TO BE NOTICED OUT HERE!

BY WHAT, SNOWMEN?
HA HA HA HA
SHROMPH, YOU FOOLS, NOT SNOWMEN! NASTY CRITTERS WITH RAZOR-SHARP TEETH.
SHRIMP? OUT HERE?
OH YES, LAUGH IT UP WHILE YA STILL CAN.

MR. KLAUS AIN'T YER AVERAGE COLLECTOR OF EXOTIC ANIMALS, NO SIR. HE FANCIES HIMSELF TO BE A TAXIDERMIST, AND BETWEEN YOU AND ME, HE AIN'T A VERY GOOD ONE.
HELLO, CHICKENHARE.
WHAT IN THE...
I NEED YOU TO HELP ME.
HEY, ABE, CHECK OUT THIS FUNNY-LOOKING GOAT OVER HERE.

WHERE?
RIGHT OVER THERE.
THAT'S WEIRD. I COULD HAVE SWORN I SAW A GOAT WEARING A TOP HAT.
THIS GUY'S GONNA GUT YA BOTH, AND THEN STUFF YA FULL'A FLUFF!
AFTER THAT, HE'LL DRESS YA UP REAL PRETTY.
HMM...
OH, I'M SORRY! WERE YOU STILL TALKING?

GRRRRRRR!
I HOPE HE TORTURES BOTH OF YA BEFORE HE KILLS YA.
NOW, DO YOU REALLY WANT THAT ON YOUR CONSCIENCE?
I SURE WOULDN'T.
MAYBE HE'LL EVEN LET ME HELP.
YOU SMELL LIKE CHEESE, MR. BARLEY.

WHY DON'T MY PETS RETURN MY LOVE, FINGERBONES?
PERHAPS, SIR, IT'S BECAUSE THEY'VE ALL BEEN STUFFED?
WELL, THEY DON'T LEAVE ME MUCH CHOICE, **DO THEY?** IT'S THE ONLY WAY I CAN BE **SURE** THEY WON'T LEAVE ME...
LIKE **HE** DID.

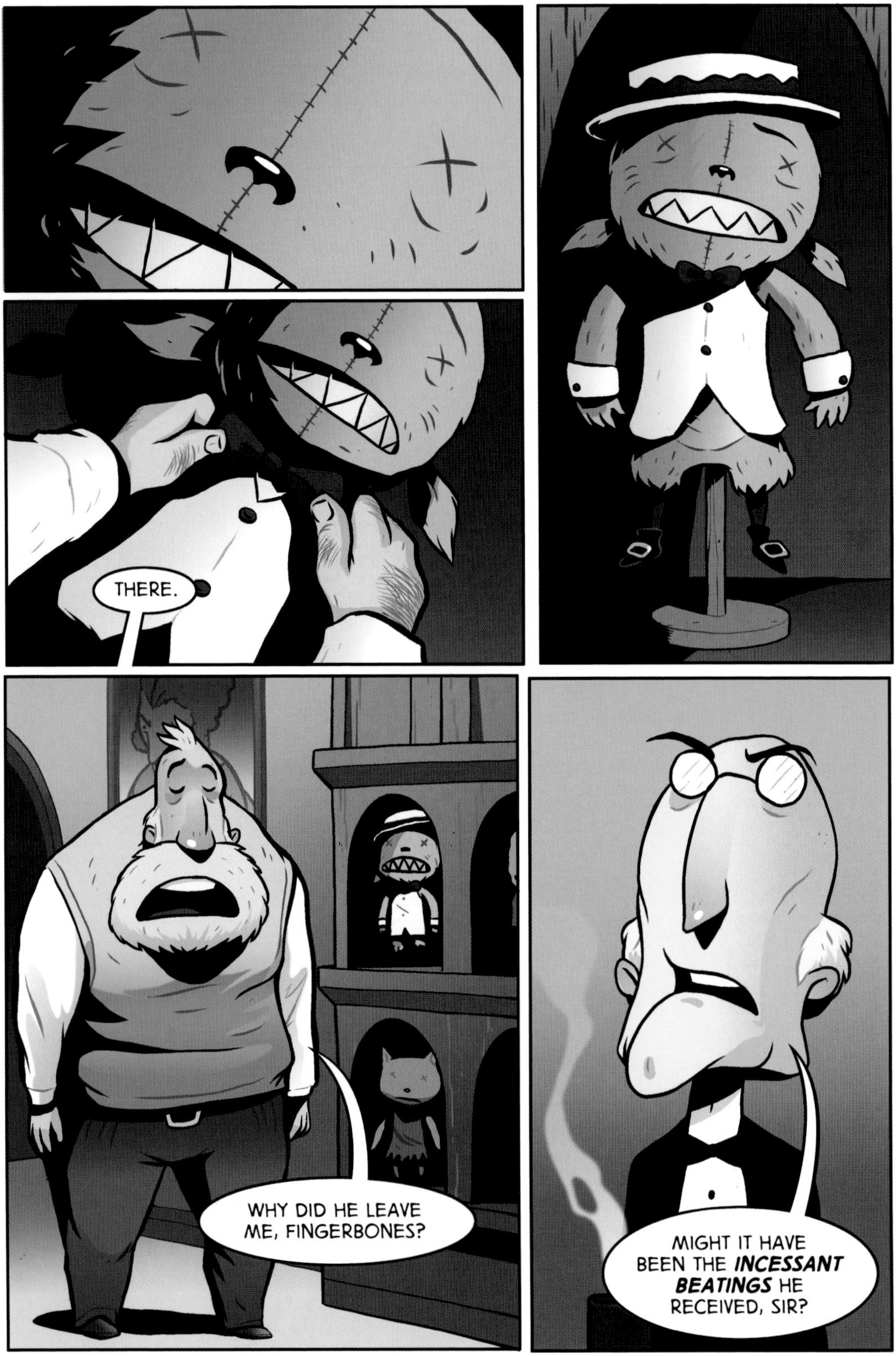
THERE.
WHY DID HE LEAVE ME, FINGERBONES?
MIGHT IT HAVE BEEN THE INCESSANT BEATINGS HE RECEIVED, SIR?

POOR LITTLE MR. BUTTONS. HOW I LOVED TO DRESS HIM UP ALL FANCY.
DO YOU THINK HE'S STILL OUT THERE SOMEWHERE, FINGERBONES?
NOT LIKELY, SIR. IT'S BEEN NEARLY FORTY YEARS.
HAS IT BEEN THAT LONG?
IT SEEMS LIKE ONLY YESTERDAY I WAS BEATING HIM FOR EATING THE BUTTONS OFF MY BEST JACKET.

BUTTONS WERE HIS ***FAVORITE.***

HE'S THE ONLY ONE THAT EVER GOT AWAY FROM ME.

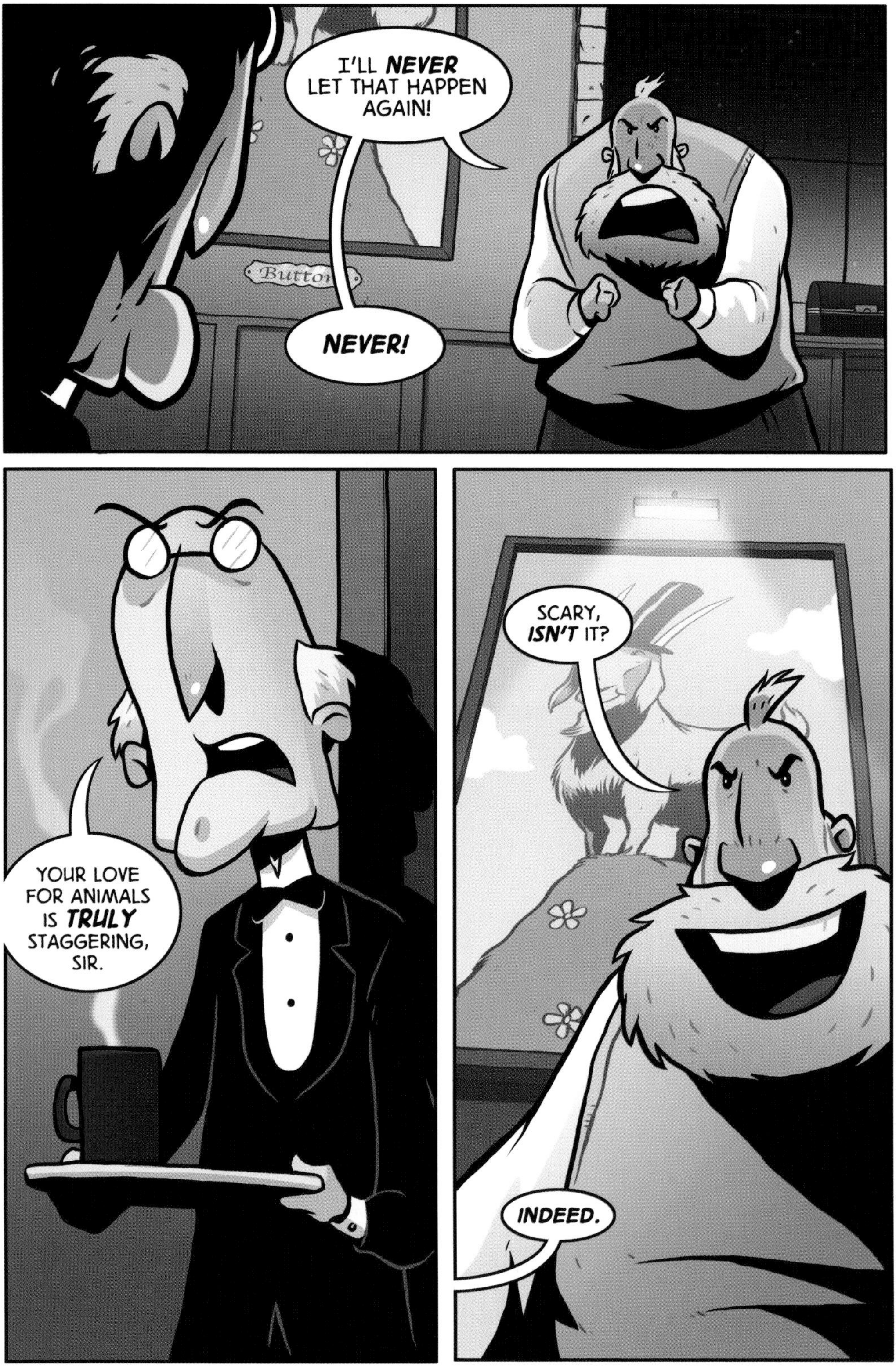
I'LL NEVER LET THAT HAPPEN AGAIN!
Button
NEVER!
YOUR LOVE FOR ANIMALS IS TRULY STAGGERING, SIR.
SCARY, ISN'T IT?
INDEED.

DO YOU THINK THIS KLAUS GUY IS **REALLY** GONNA STUFF US, CHICKENHARE?
MAYBE HE WON'T EVEN WANT US, ABE.
NOT LIKELY.
THIS FELLA'S INTO THE RARE AND EXOTIC STUFF.
AND YOU TWO'RE 'BOUT AS RARE AND EXOTIC AS I'VE SEEN.

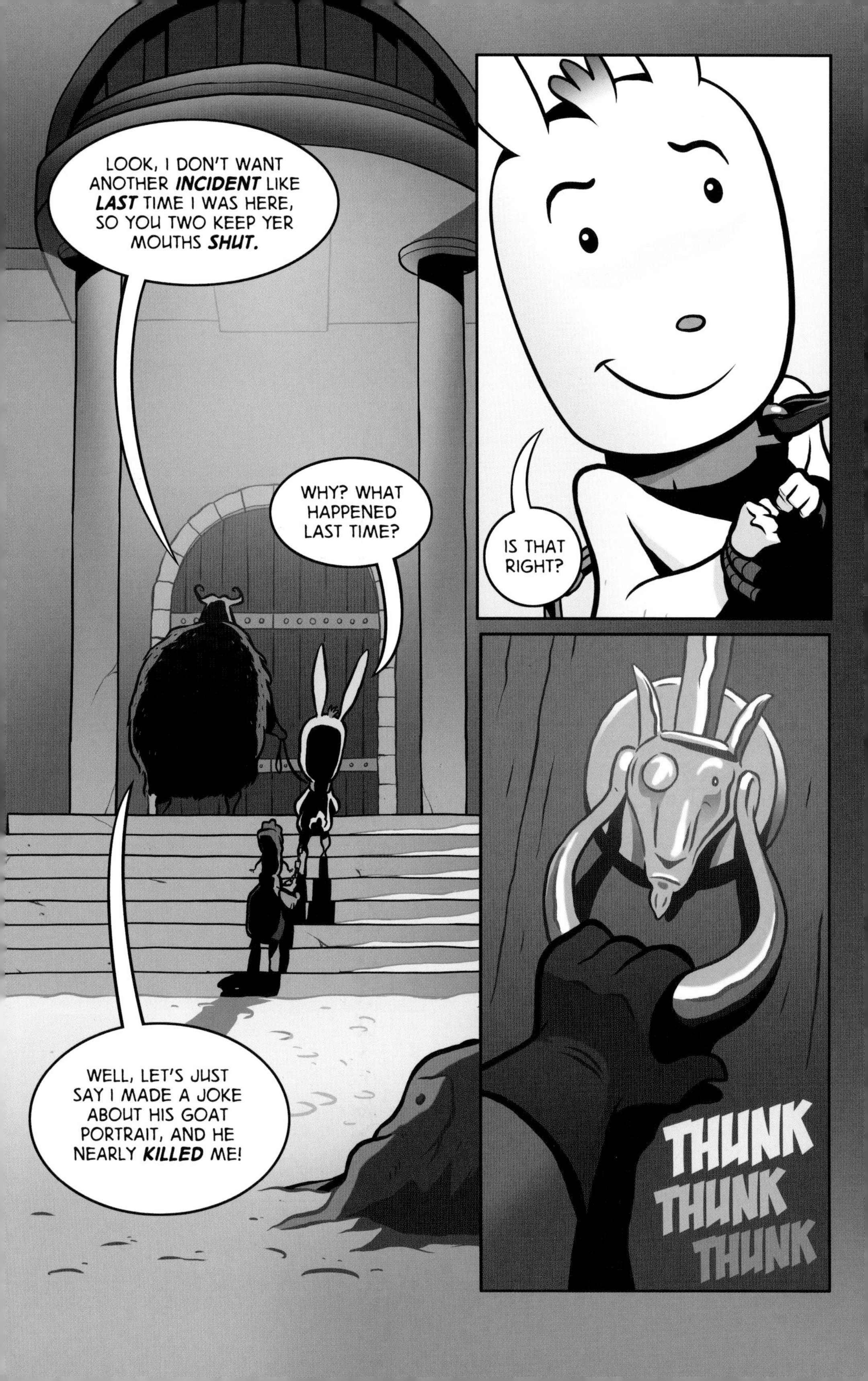
LOOK, I DON'T WANT ANOTHER INCIDENT LIKE LAST TIME I WAS HERE, SO YOU TWO KEEP YER MOUTHS SHUT.
WHY? WHAT HAPPENED LAST TIME?
WELL, LET'S JUST SAY I MADE A JOKE ABOUT HIS GOAT PORTRAIT, AND HE NEARLY KILLED ME!
IS THAT RIGHT?
THUNK
THUNK
THUNK

ARE YOU EXPECTING GUESTS, SIR?
IT'S BARLEY. AND HE'S LATE.
SHOW HIM IN HERE, FINGERBONES.
VERY GOOD, SIR.
KLAK

BE A GOOD BUTLER, FINGERBONES. GO TELL KLAUS I'M HERE.
HE ALREADY **KNOWS**, AND HE INFORMS ME YOU ARE **QUITE** LATE.
IS HE MAD?
AS A **HATTER.**

YOU'RE **LATE**, BARLEY!
S-SORRY, MR. KLAUS.
LET'S TALK IN THE DRAWING ROOM.
THANK YOU, MR. KLAUS.
NOT A PEEP!
UNDERSTAND?
COMPLETELY.
YEP.

HEY, BARLEY, IS THAT THE PORTRAIT?
YEP, THAT'S THE ONE, AND I...
...THOUGHT I TOLD YOU TO KEEP QUIET!
IS THIS IT, BARLEY?
THIS LOOKS LIKE A RABBIT AND A STUPID TURTLE TO ME. NOTHING RARE OR EXOTIC ABOUT EITHER OF THEM!

ON THE **CONTRARY**, KLAUS.
THESE ARE LIKE NO ANIMALS YOU'VE **EVER** SEEN BEFORE!
I'M LISTENING.
TAKE THIS ONE, FOR EXAMPLE.
THIS IS NO ORDINARY TURTLE. THIS IS A RARE WHISKERED CHELONAI! MORE COMMONLY KNOWN AS THE BEARDED BOX TURTLE, AND THE ONLY ONE KNOWN TO EXIST!

THAT'S THE SORRIEST EXCUSE FOR AN EXOTIC ANIMAL I'VE EVER **SEEN!**
MOVING RIGHT ALONG. I THINK YOU'RE **REALLY** GONNA **LOVE** THIS NEXT ONE.
FLING
GET AWAY FROM ME, **PIG!**
I LIKE **THIS** ONE BETTER **ALREADY!**

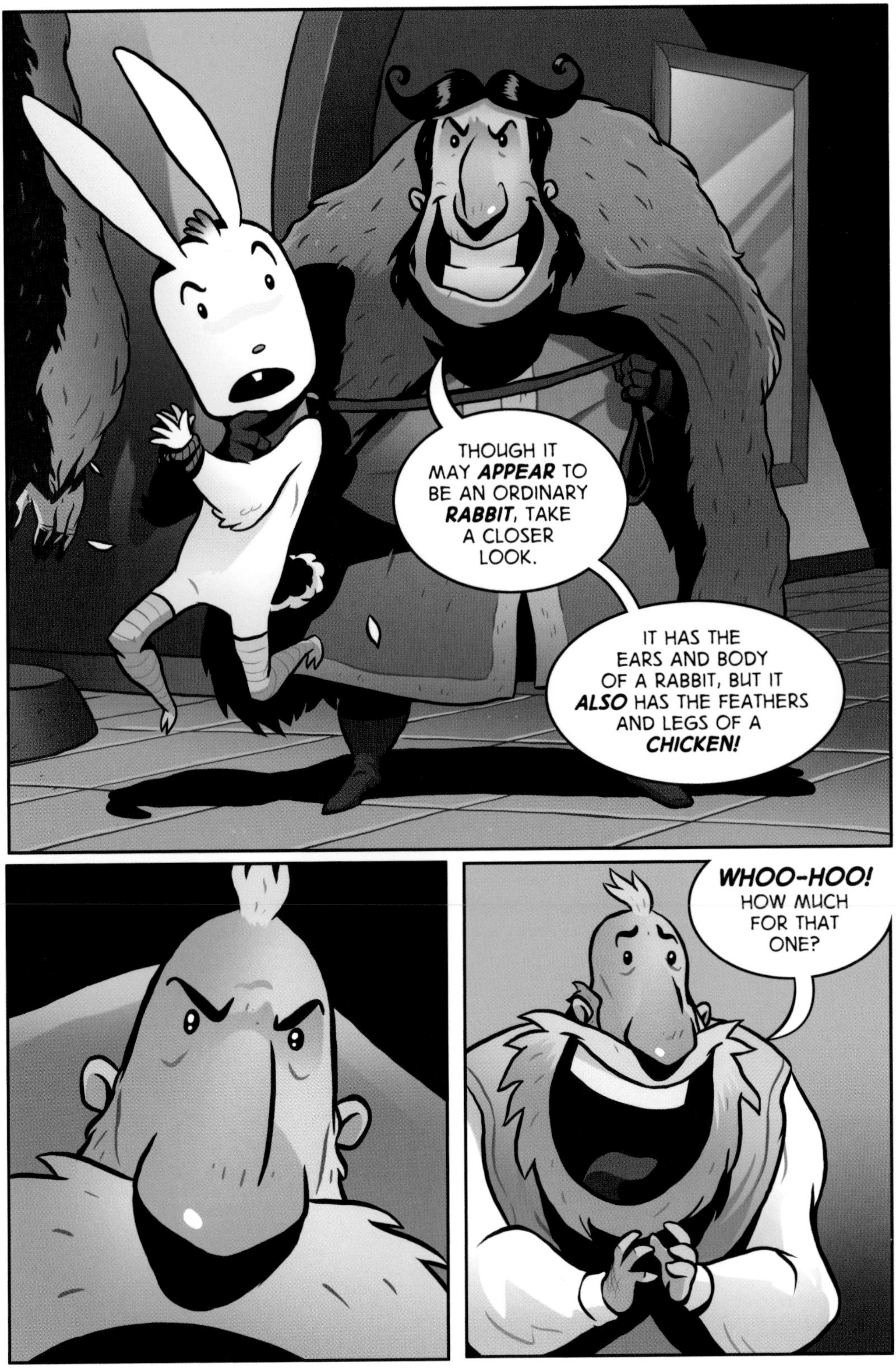
THOUGH IT MAY **APPEAR** TO BE AN ORDINARY **RABBIT**, TAKE A CLOSER LOOK.
IT HAS THE EARS AND BODY OF A RABBIT, BUT IT **ALSO** HAS THE FEATHERS AND LEGS OF A **CHICKEN!**
WHOO-HOO! HOW MUCH FOR THAT ONE?

ABE, ARE YOU HURT?
JUST MY FEELINGS.
I'M AFRAID THEY ONLY COME AS A PAIR, AND THEY **WON'T** BE CHEAP.
GOOD, BECAUSE I'M READY TO LEAVE.
I HAVE AN IDEA. BE READY TO RUN WHEN I TELL YOU TO, OKAY?

EXCUSE ME, MR. KLAUS?
WHAT ARE YOU DOING?
YES, MY LITTLE CHICKEN-BUNNY?
I JUST WANTED TO TELL YOU THAT I DON'T THINK YOUR GOAT PORTRAIT IS NEARLY AS GUT-WRENCHINGLY HIDEOUS AS MR. BARLEY WAS TELLING US IT WAS.
YOU'RE WELCOME.

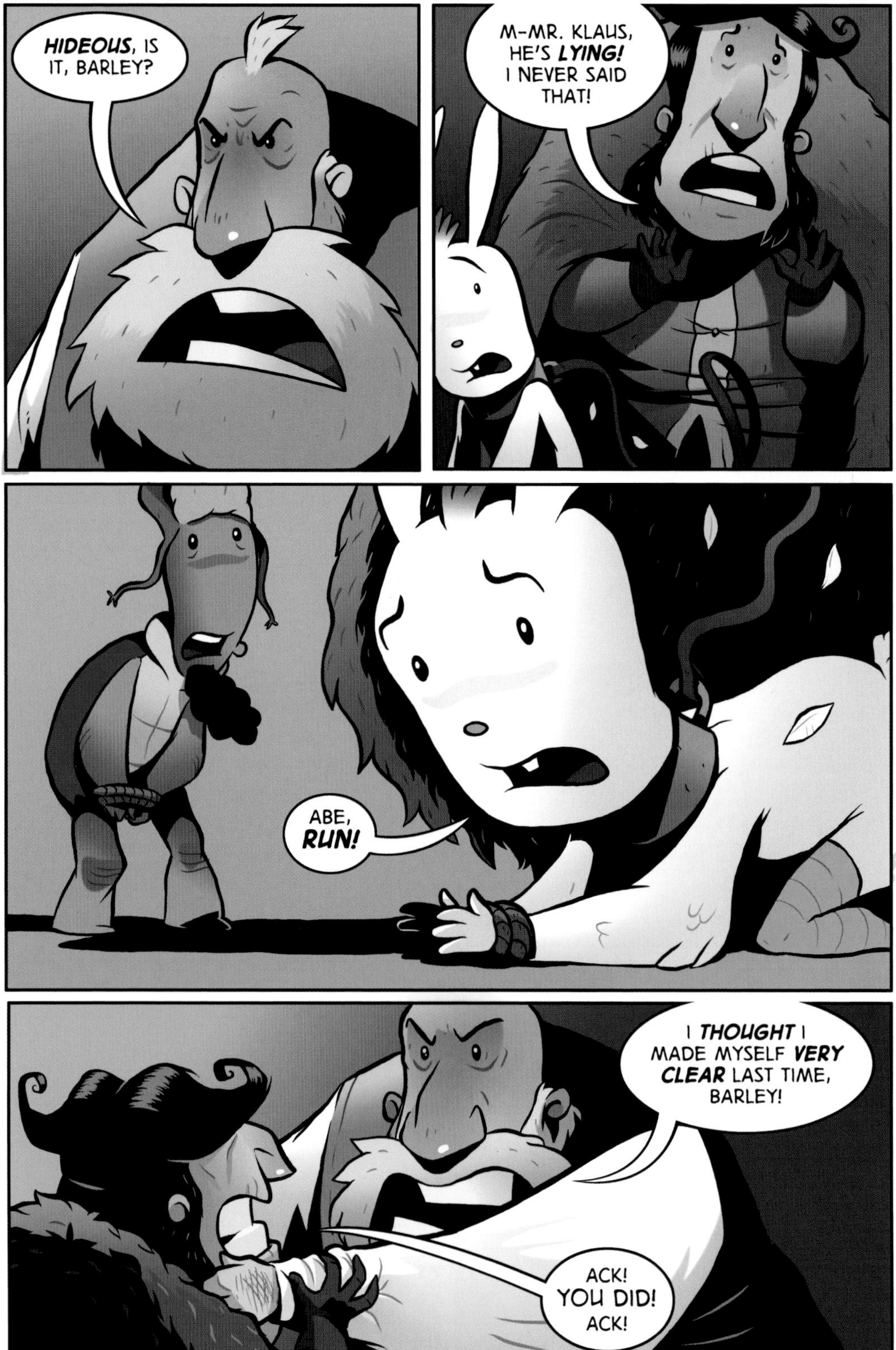
HIDEOUS, IS IT, BARLEY?
M-MR. KLAUS, HE'S LYING! I NEVER SAID THAT!
ABE, RUN!
I THOUGHT I MADE MYSELF VERY CLEAR LAST TIME, BARLEY!
ACK! YOU DID! ACK!

I CAN'T **BELIEVE** YOU JUST DID THAT!
I CAN'T BELIEVE IT **WORKED!**
WUMP

THUMP
WHO PUT THAT BRICK WALL THERE...?
AND JUST *WHERE* DO YOU TWO THINK YOU'RE GOING?
CHICKENHARE?
ARE YOU OKAY?
LEAVE HIM ALONE!
STOP!
TAKE THEM UPSTAIRS, PLUMMS.

I THINK YOUR BUDDY'S WAKING UP.
HEY, CHICKENHARE.
CHICKENHARE, ARE YOU HURT?
ABE? WHAT HAPPENED? WHERE ARE WE?
THEY PUT US IN CAGES...
...AND I THINK THAT JUST ABOUT COVERS IT.
WE NEED TO GET *OUTTA* HERE!
WELL, BY *ALL* MEANS, DON'T LET A LITTLE THING LIKE THAT *METAL CAGE* STOP YA.

WHO'S THIS GUY?
THAT'S BANJO. HE'S KIND OF A JERK.

WOW, THAT HURTS, ABE.
AND THAT'S MEG OVER THERE.
I GET THE FEELING SHE DOESN'T CARE MUCH FOR HIM, EITHER.

HOW LONG HAVE THE TWO OF YOU BEEN HERE?
I'VE ACTUALLY LOST TRACK.
HAVE YOU TRIED TO ESCAPE?
ONLY EVERY SINGLE DAY SINCE I **GOT** HERE, CHICKEN-LEGS!

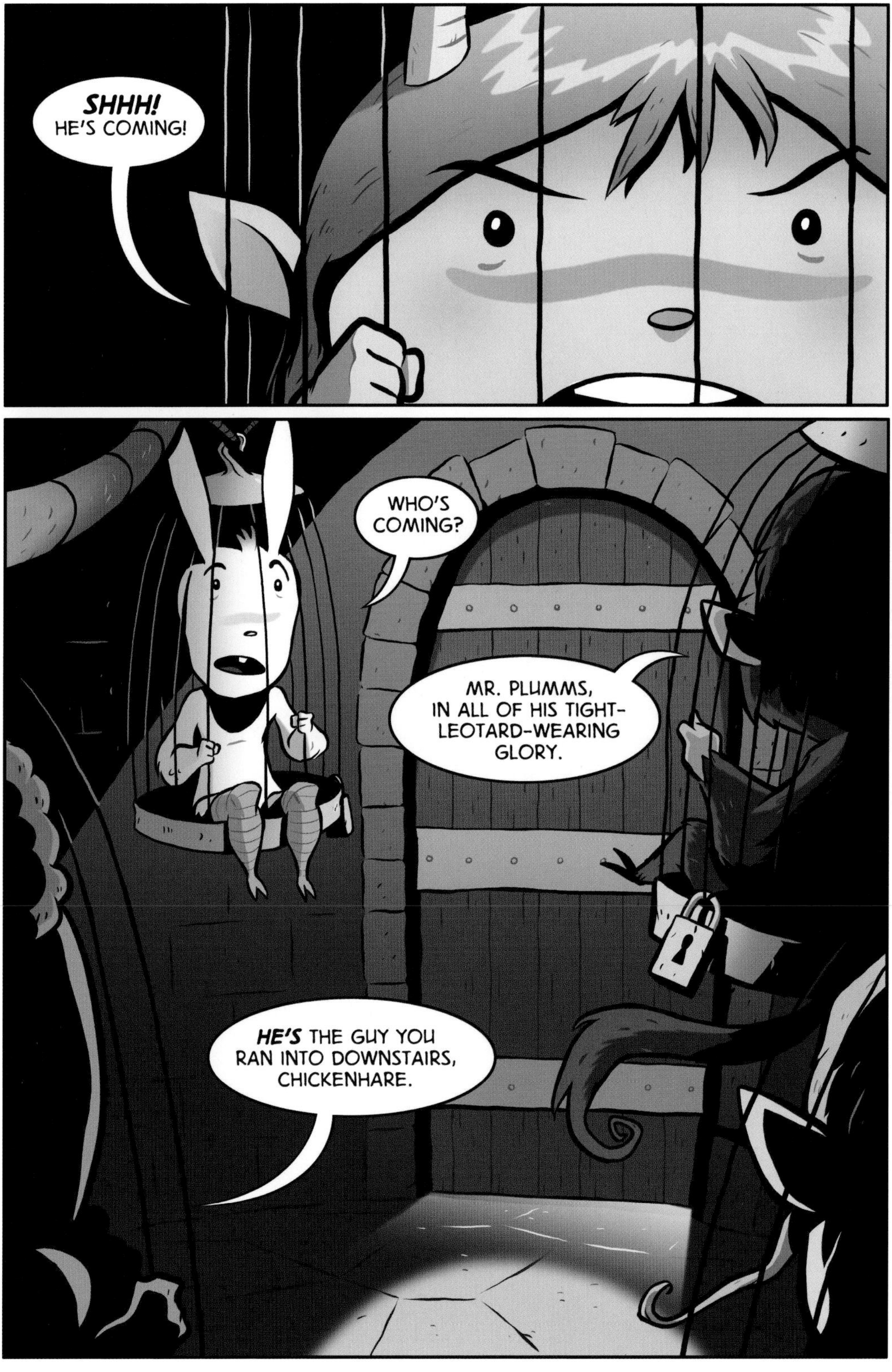
SHHH! HE'S COMING!
WHO'S COMING?
MR. PLUMMS, IN ALL OF HIS TIGHT-LEOTARD-WEARING GLORY.
HE'S THE GUY YOU RAN INTO DOWNSTAIRS, CHICKENHARE.

BADOOM
WELL, WELL, WELL. LOOK WHO'S ***FINALLY*** AWAKE.
I ***DEMAND*** THAT YOU RELEASE US!
UM... CHICKENHARE, MAYBE YOU SHOULD PLAY NICE.
BETTER ***LISTEN*** TO YOUR FRIENDS, CHICKENHARE. IT WOULD BE A SHAME IF I HAD TO ***HURT*** SOMEBODY.

I DOUBT MR. KLAUS WOULD WANT YOU HURTING HIS FAVORITE NEW PET, TUBBY.
SLAP
NOW LET US OUT!
YOU'RE RIGHT, I CAN'T HURT YOU...
...BUT I CAN HURT YOUR GREEN BUDDY OVER THERE.

WAIT! PLUMMS, HOLD ON!
I'M SORRY!
TOO LATE!
CLANG

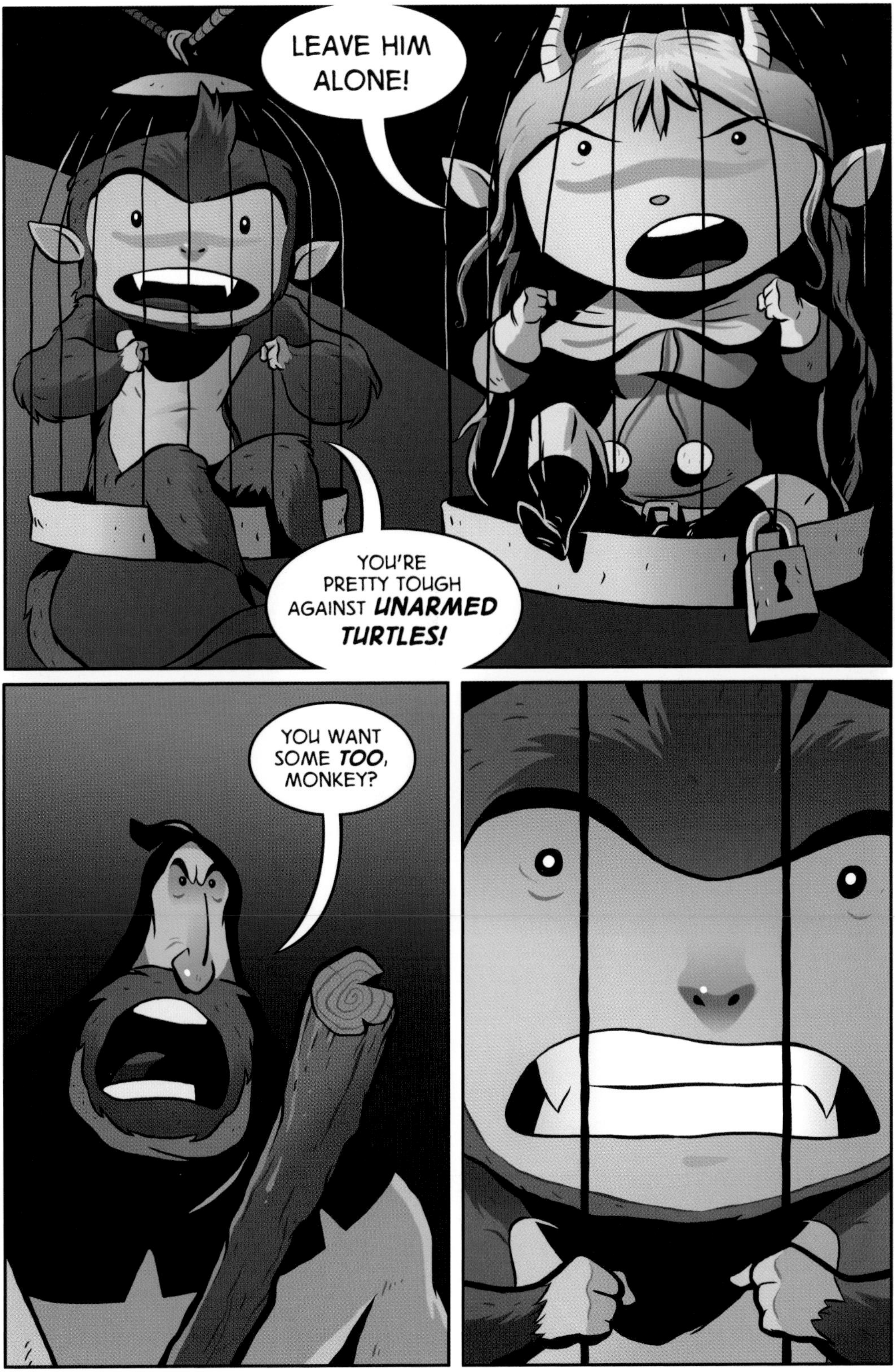
LEAVE HIM ALONE!
YOU'RE PRETTY TOUGH AGAINST *UNARMED TURTLES!*
YOU WANT SOME *TOO*, MONKEY?

I'LL BE BACK FOR THE TURTLE REAL SOON. HE'S GOT A DATE WITH THE TAXIDERMIST.
STINKS TO BE YOU, GREENY!
AND YOU'RE NEXT, MONKEY!
BADOOM
WE GOTTA GET OUTTA HERE!
ABE, I'M SO SORRY. ARE YOU OKAY?
I'LL TELL YA WHEN THE ROOM STOPS SPINNING.

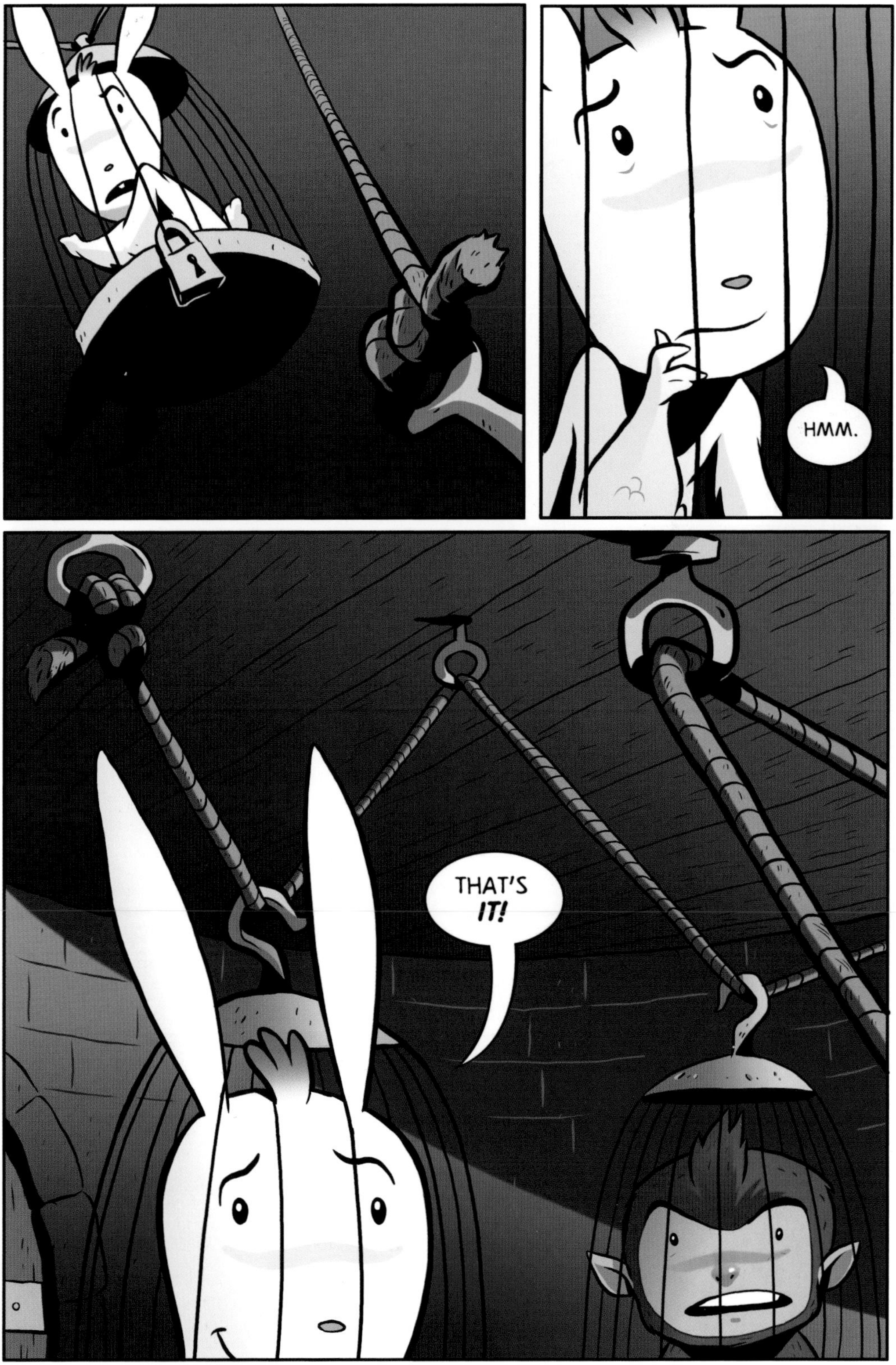
HMM.
THAT'S *IT!*

I KNOW HOW TO *FREE* US!
HEY, LOOK AT THIS.
THE *ROPE!* IF WE CAN UNTIE IT, WE CAN *ESCAPE!*
UH...GUYS?
YEAH, I FIGURED *THAT* OUT ABOUT TWO SECONDS AFTER I GOT HERE! WE CAN'T *REACH* IT.
YOU GUYS AREN'T GONNA BELIEVE THIS!
ABE! LET THE ADULTS TALK, OKAY?

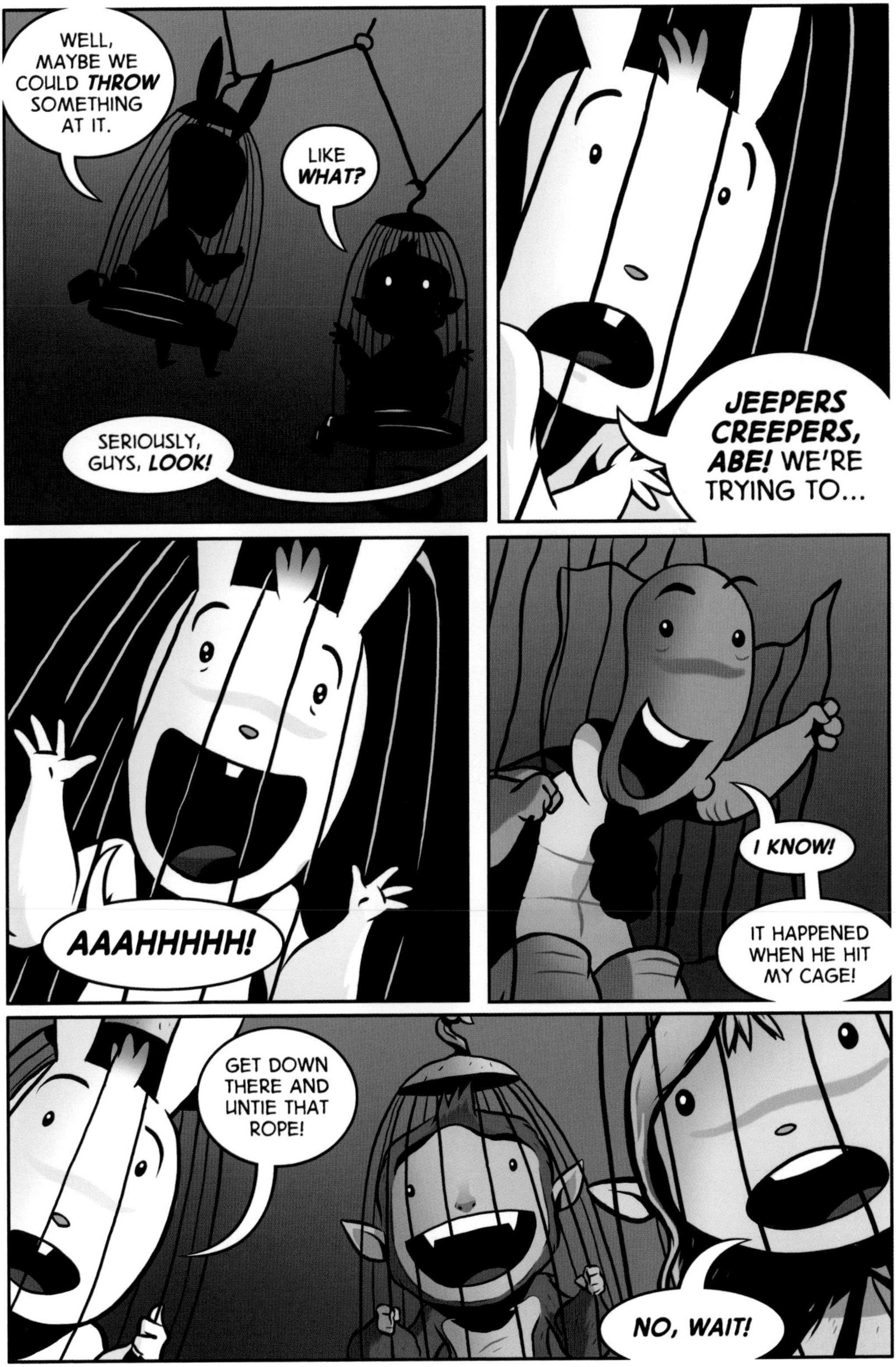
WELL, MAYBE WE COULD THROW SOMETHING AT IT.
LIKE WHAT?
SERIOUSLY, GUYS, LOOK!
JEEPERS CREEPERS, ABE! WE'RE TRYING TO...
AAAHHHHH!
I KNOW!
IT HAPPENED WHEN HE HIT MY CAGE!
GET DOWN THERE AND UNTIE THAT ROPE!
NO, WAIT!

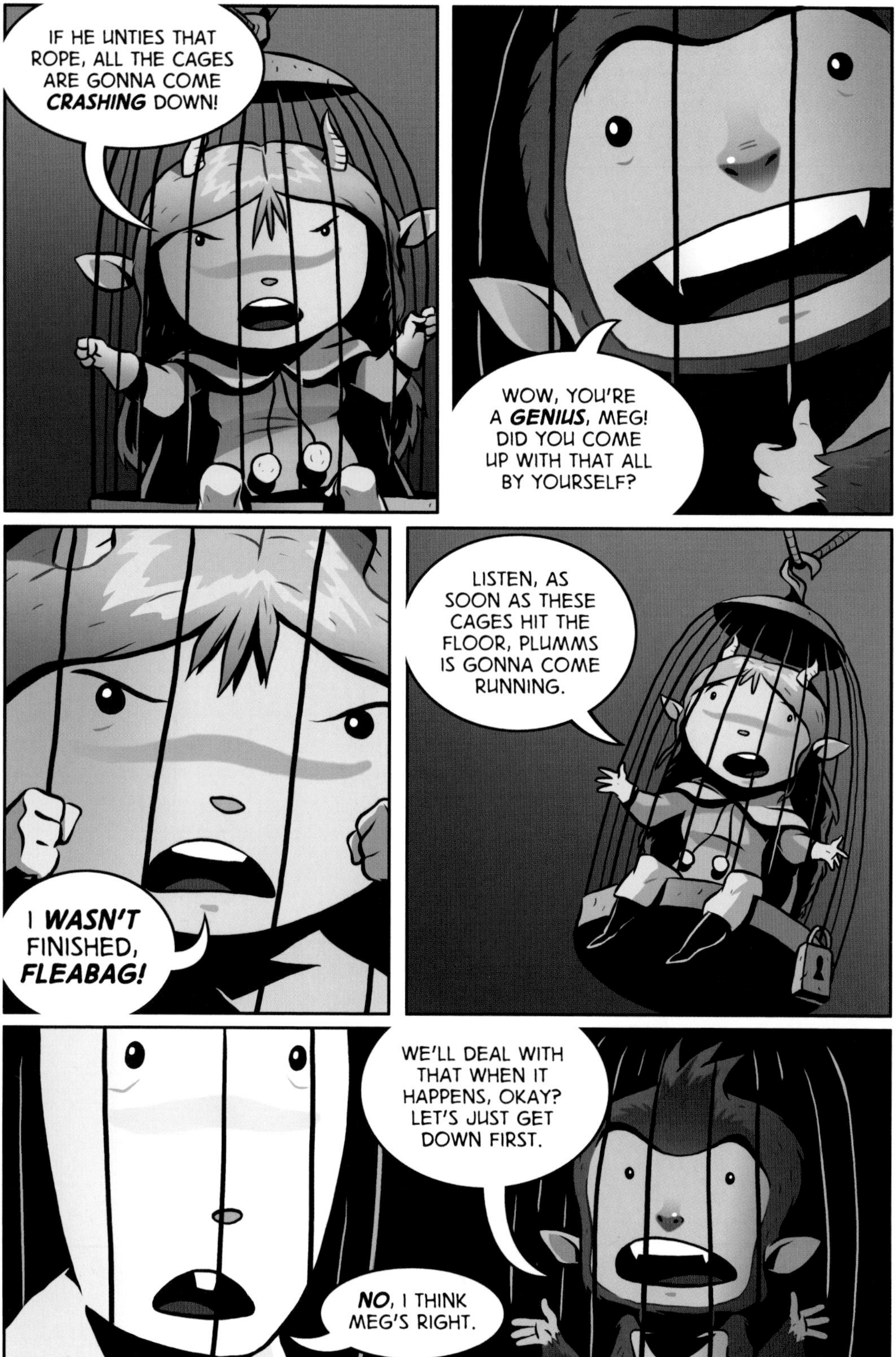
IF HE UNTIES THAT ROPE, ALL THE CAGES ARE GONNA COME *CRASHING* DOWN!
WOW, YOU'RE A *GENIUS*, MEG! DID YOU COME UP WITH THAT ALL BY YOURSELF?
I *WASN'T* FINISHED, *FLEABAG!*
LISTEN, AS SOON AS THESE CAGES HIT THE FLOOR, PLUMMS IS GONNA COME RUNNING.
WE'LL DEAL WITH THAT WHEN IT HAPPENS, OKAY? LET'S JUST GET DOWN FIRST.
NO, I THINK MEG'S RIGHT.

OKAY, SO AFTER WE'RE DOWN, ABE, YOU GRAB THE KEYS AND OPEN OUR CAGES.
GOTCHA.
WHAT CAN I DO?
MEG, I'LL NEED YOU TO HELP ME WITH THAT WINDOW.
WHOA! WHAT'S ALL THIS TALK ABOUT LETTING HER OUT?
WHY WOULDN'T WE LET MEG OUT?
BECAUSE IF YOU LET HER OUT, SHE'S GONNA TRY TO KILL ME. THAT'S WHY.

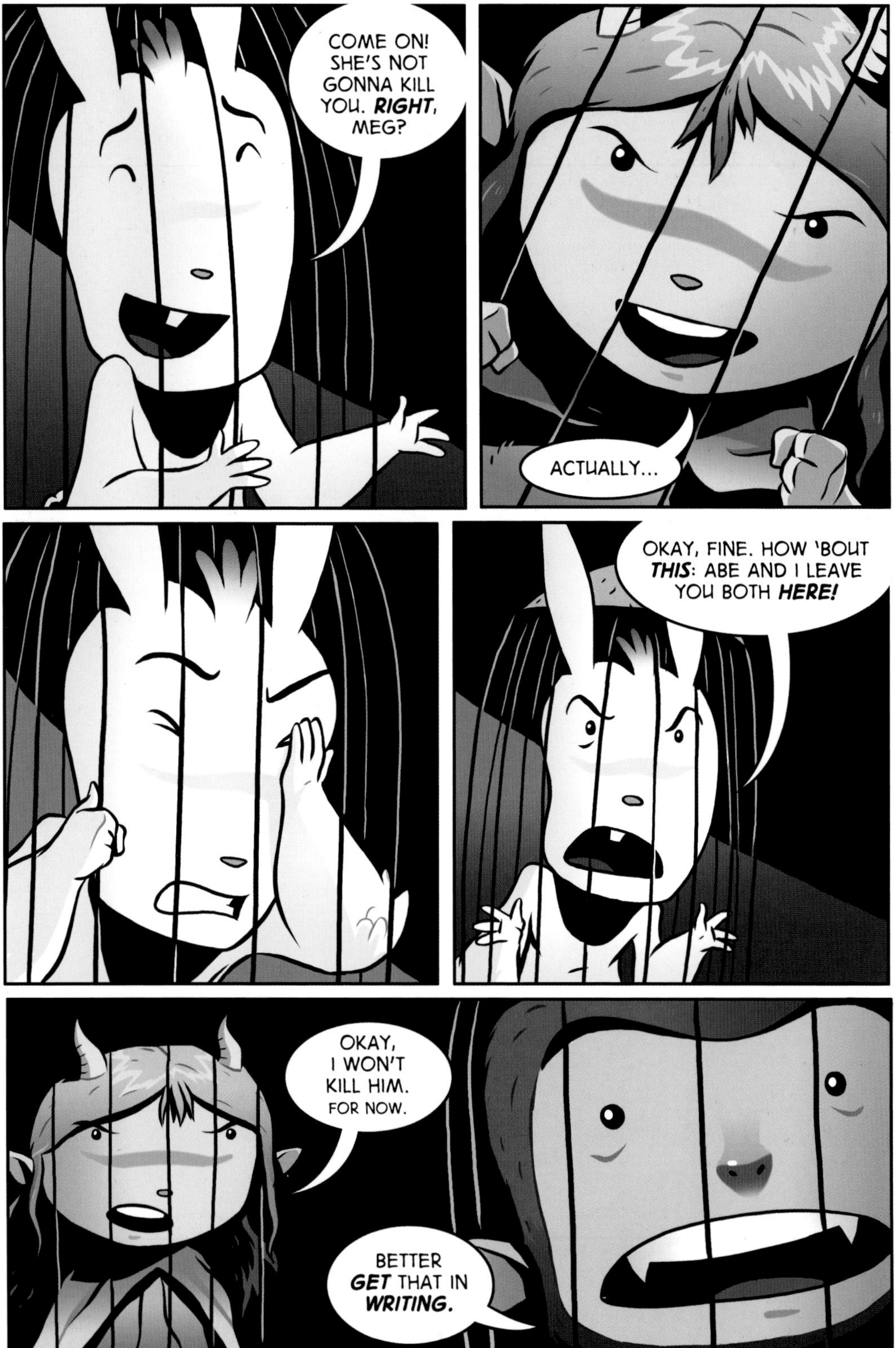
COME ON! SHE'S NOT GONNA KILL YOU. ***RIGHT***, MEG?
ACTUALLY...
OKAY, FINE. HOW 'BOUT ***THIS***: ABE AND I LEAVE YOU BOTH ***HERE!***
OKAY, I WON'T KILL HIM. FOR NOW.
BETTER ***GET*** THAT IN ***WRITING.***

THAT'S RIGHT, MR. SMILES-A-LOT. DADDY HAS TWO NEW BROTHERS AND A SISTER FOR YOU TO PLAY WITH.
IT **WOULD** HAVE BEEN **FOUR**, BUT I'VE DECIDED TO MAKE THE **TURTLE** INTO AN ASHTRAY.

WHO'S DADDY'S FAVORITE WIDDLE BEAR?
EXCUSE ME, MR. KLAUS.
WHAT IS IT, PLUMMS?
I THOUGHT YOU'D LIKE TO KNOW THE RABBIT THING IS AWAKE.
THANK YOU. PREPARE THE OPERATING ROOM.
I'VE DECIDED TO DO HIM FIRST AFTER ALL.
WITH ***PLEASURE***, SIR.

CLANG
CLUNG
BOOM
WHAT IN THE...?
BETTER NOT BE MAKING A ***MESS*** UP THERE!
CRASSHH

BADOOM
WHAT'S GOING ON IN HERE?!
NO!
NO!
NO!
NO!
NO!
NO!
NO!

THIS ISN'T HAPPENING! THEY MUST HAVE GONE OUT THE WINDOW!
HEY, WAIT A SECOND! THERE'S NO WAY THEY COULD ESCAPE OUT THAT WINDOW.
IT'S A FORTY-FOOT DROP.

WELL, LOOKY WHAT I FOUND OUT HERE ON THIS TINY LEDGE.
SO MUCH FOR THAT BIG ESCAPE PLAN, HUH?
WHY DON'T YOU JUST COME BACK INSIDE. THERE'S NOWHERE ELSE TO GO EXCEPT DOWN, AND I DOUBT YOU WANNA GO THAT WAY.

WUMP

AAHHH!
WHEN I TOLD YOU TO KNOCK HIM OUT, I DIDN'T MEAN OUT THE ***WINDOW!***
I IMPROVISED.

DADDY HAS TO GO TO WORK NOW, SO...

NOW WHAT?
WELL, I GUESS WE SHOULD FIND ANOTHER WAY OUT.
I THINK THE MAIN ENTRANCE IS JUST DOWNSTAIRS.
SOMEBODY'S COMING!
QUICK, BEHIND THE DOOR!
WHAT'S GOING ON IN HERE?!
NO!

NOOOOOO!
CCRREEEAAK

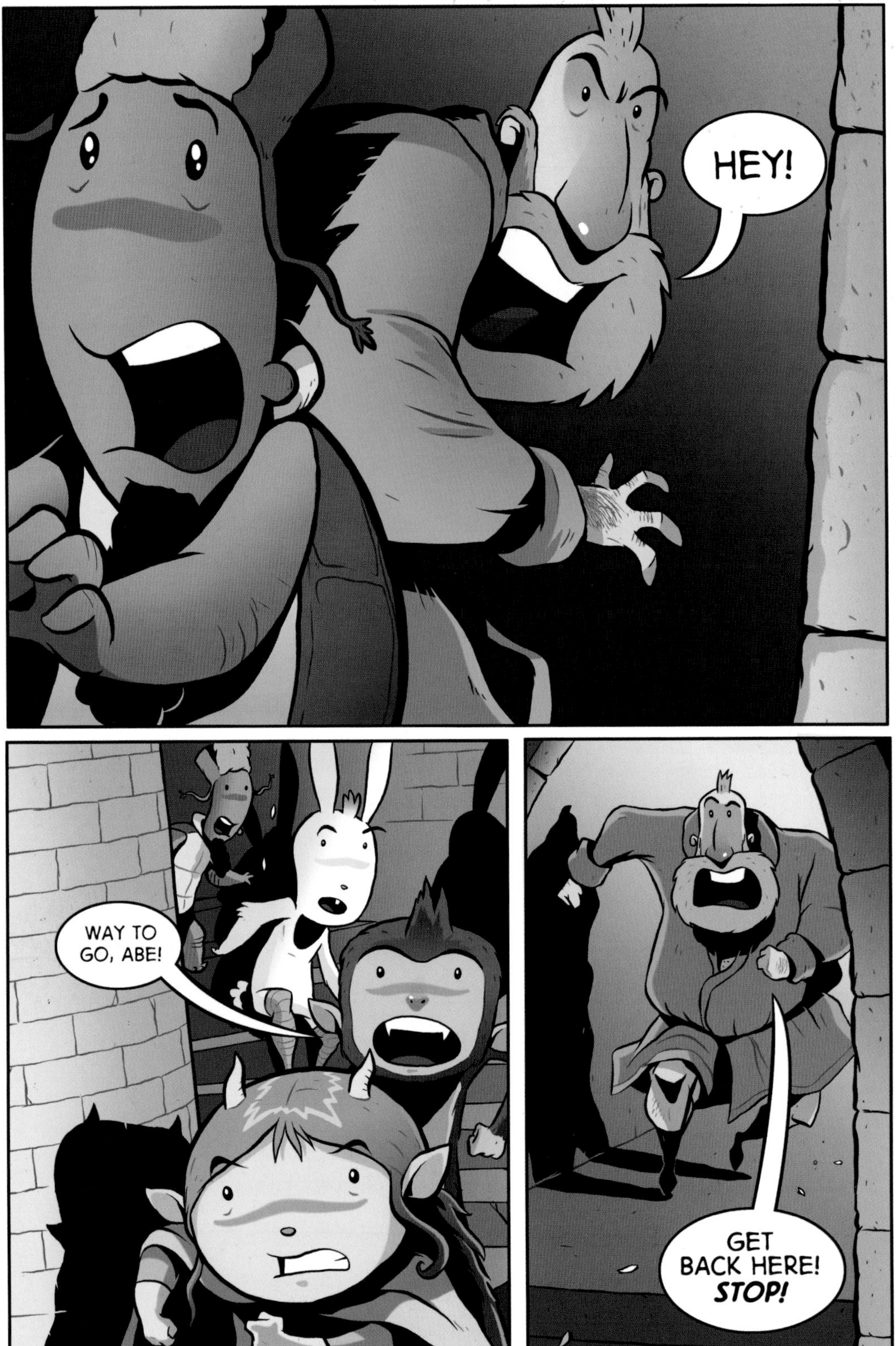
HEY!
WAY TO GO, ABE!
GET BACK HERE! STOP!

WAIT.

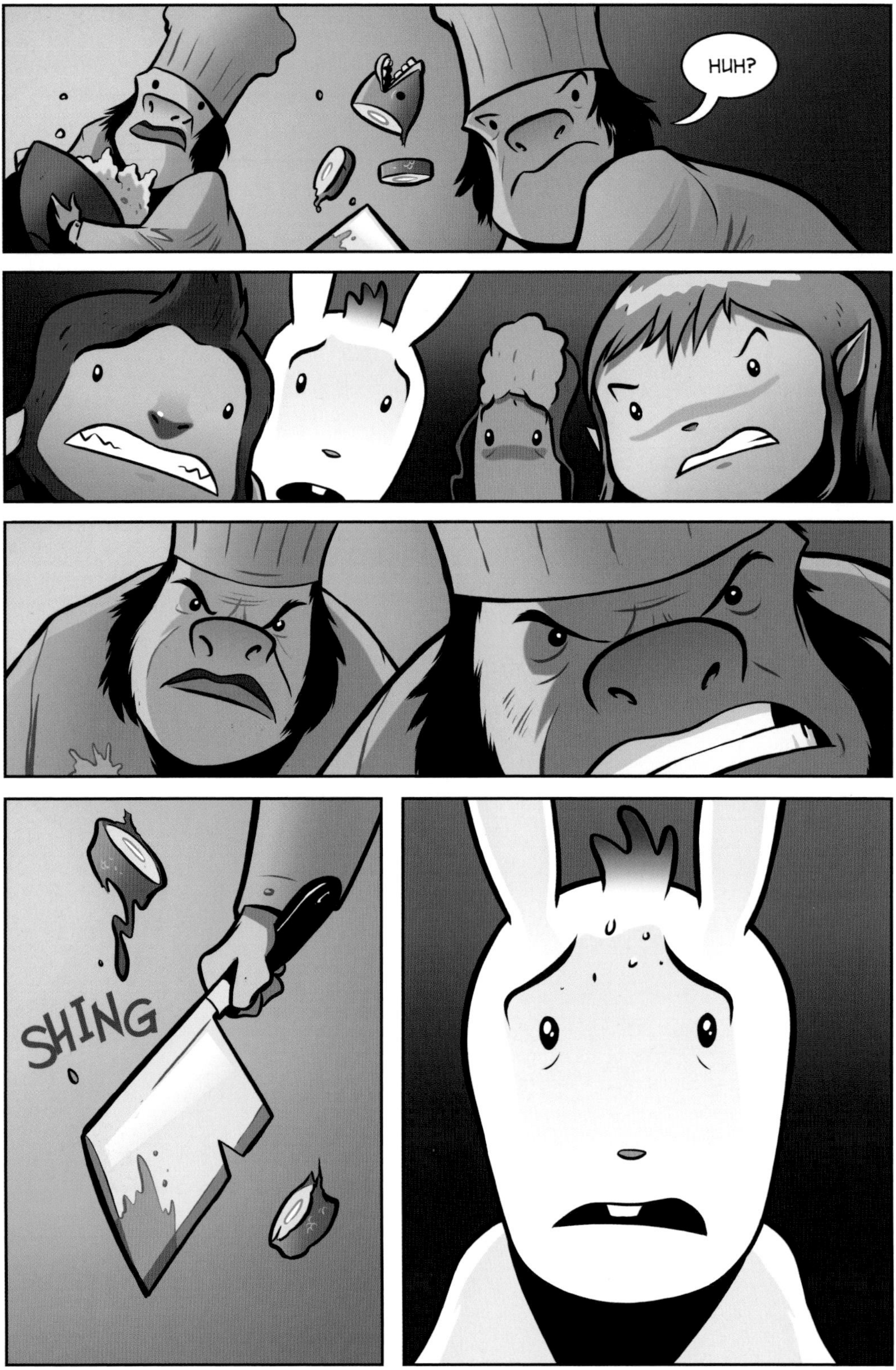
HUH?
SHING

RUN!
I AM!
FASTER!
FASTER!
FASTER!
DOWN HERE!

OH NO, IT'S FINGERBONES!
YOU **VERMIN** AREN'T GOING **ANYWHERE!**

MEG! BANJO! THAT'S ENOUGH! WE NEED TO GO!
THIS IS YOUR LUCKY DAY, ***BUTLER!***
COME ON!

I WON'T LET YOU LEAVE ME!
SIR! WAIT!
WHOA!
OW! MY LEGS!

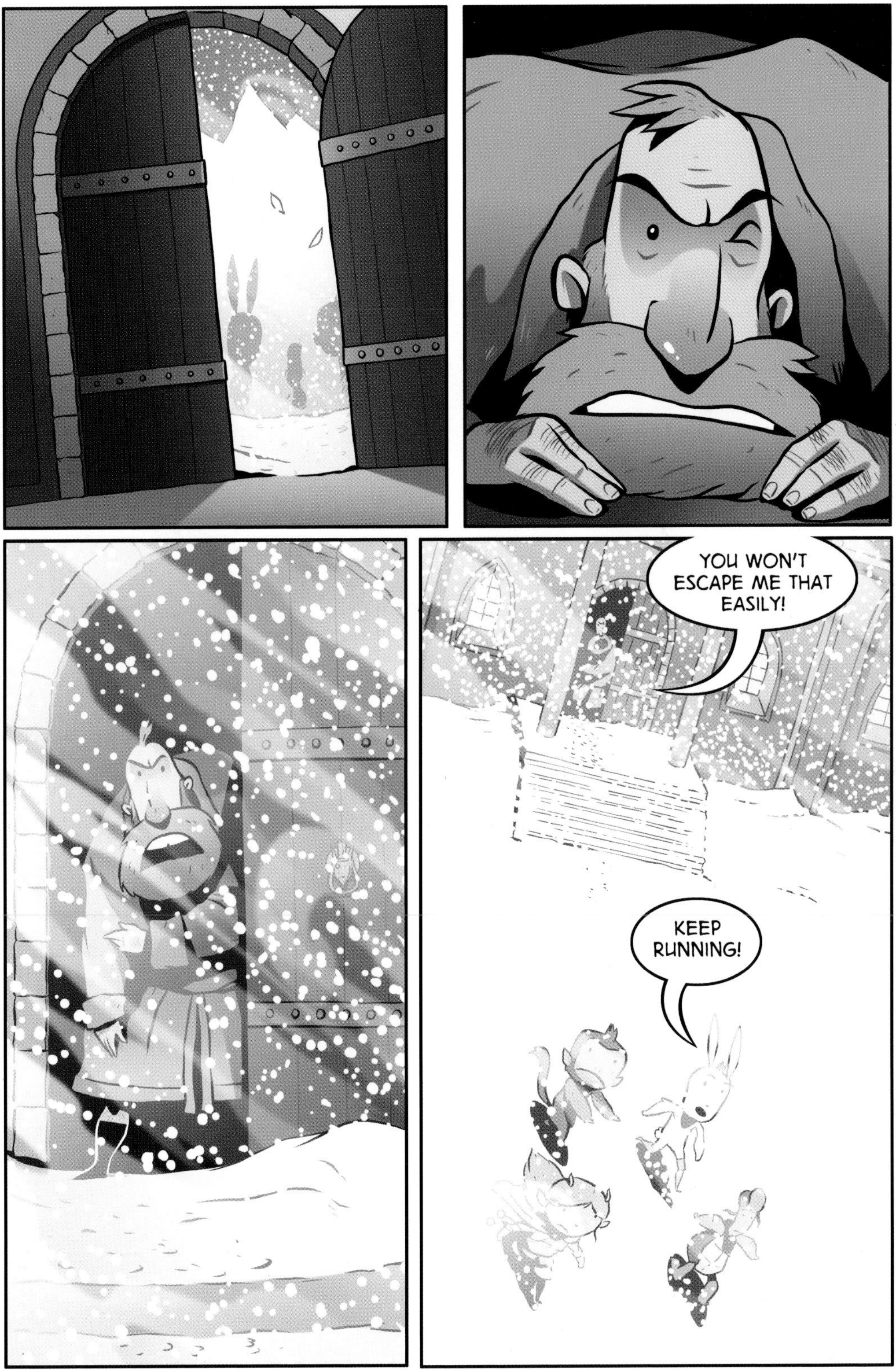
YOU WON'T ESCAPE ME THAT EASILY!
KEEP RUNNING!

AT LEAST IT'S FINALLY STOPPED SNOWING.
IS IT A TAD COLDER THAN YOU'RE USED TO, DEVIL?
HMM-HMM-HM-HMM
I'M FINE, THANKS.
HOW ARE YOU STAYIN' SO CHIPPER, ABE?
IT'S *FREEZING* OUT HERE!
MY *HAT* AND THESE *SWEET GLOVES* ARE KEEPING ME *TOASTY!*
YOU DON'T SAY?

YOU ARE SO RIGHT ABOUT THESE GLOVES, ABE. THEY *ARE* TOASTY!
SHUT UP!
JUST SAY THE WORD, ABE, AND HE'S DEAD.
YOU *ARE* A JERK!
HEY, I *LET* HIM KEEP THE HAT.
ONLY BECAUSE IT DIDN'T *FIT!*
THANKS ANYWAY, MEG. IT'S NOT WORTH KILLING HIM OVER MY GLOVES.
I'LL LEAVE IT ON THE TABLE, JUST IN CASE YOU CHANGE YOUR MIND.

CHICKENHARE.
HELP ME, CHICKENHARE.
WHAT IN THE...?
YOU JUST TRY IT, MEG!
EVERYONE STAY CLOSE. IT'S GETTING WORSE OUT HERE AND WE DON'T WANT TO BE SEPARATED.
EXCEPT BANJO!
WHAT SIZE WAS THAT HAT AGAIN?

HEY, BANJO, ANY CHANCE I COULD GET THOSE GLOVES BACK?
UM... **NOPE**, PROBABLY NOT.
WHY NOT?
I GOT RID OF THEM ABOUT **FIVE** HOURS BACK.
WHAT?!
WELL, WHAT WAS I **SUPPOSED** TO DO, ABE?
MY HANDS WERE GETTING **REALLY** SWEATY AND PRUNEY.

HEY, THAT'S THE CAVE CHICKENHARE AND I PASSED ON THE WAY IN.
I THINK BARLEY SAID IT WASN'T SAFE, THOUGH. SOMETHING ABOUT SHROMPH?
WHO CARES! I'M ***FREEZING!***
WHAT DO ***YOU*** THINK WE SHOULD DO, CHICKENHARE?
HEY, WHERE IS HE?

CHICKENHARE!
CHICKENHARE!
I'M REALLY COLD AND I WANNA GO INTO THE CAVE!
C'MON, ABE. I'M SURE HE'LL SHOW UP.
WHAT DID YOU SAY LIVED IN HERE, ABE? SHRIMP?
SHROMPH, YOU IDIOT.

YOU AGAIN!
OKAY, I'M HERE. WHAT DO YOU WANT?
I NEED YOU TO *FIND* ME.
I JUST *DID!* I'M STANDING RIGHT IN FRONT OF YOU!
COME *CLOSER.*

WELL, AT LEAST I WASN'T IMAGINING THINGS EARLIER BACK ON THE...
...ROAD!

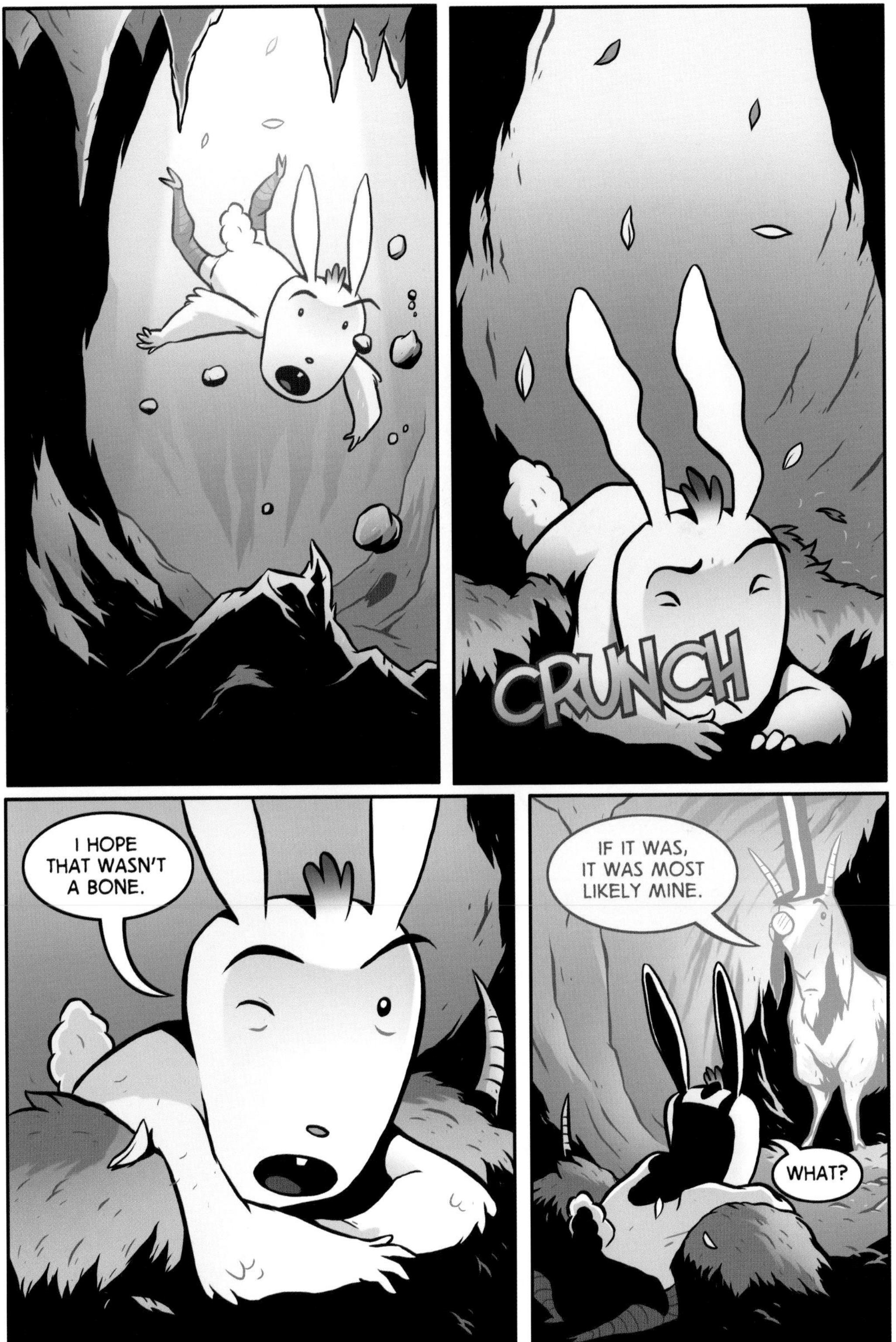
CRUNCH
I HOPE THAT WASN'T A BONE.
IF IT WAS, IT WAS MOST LIKELY MINE.
WHAT?

PLEASE, SIR. **DON'T** MAKE ME GO WITH YOU. I'M IN **UNBEARABLE** PAIN.

FASTER!
CRACK

MR. KLAUS, **PLEASE!**
FASTER, BEEF!
FASTER, PATTY!
SIR, I'M **SURE** I MUST BE BLEEDING INTERNALLY!
YOU SHOULD HAVE THOUGHT ABOUT THAT BEFORE YOU LET THEM ESCAPE!

IT'S BEEN HOURS.
I DON'T THINK HE'S COMING, ABE.

YOU GUYS DON'T THINK THAT TAXIDERMIST GUY GOT HIM, **DO** YOU?
I HOPE NOT.
JUST IN CASE, THOUGH, MAYBE WE SHOULD MOVE DEEPER INTO THE CAVE.

I THINK WE'RE ***LOST.***
AT LEAST IT'S GETTING WARMER, ***RIGHT?***
ALWAYS LOOKING ON THE BRIGHT SIDE.
I TRY.
WOULD YOU TWO LIKE TO BE ***ALONE***...
...TO ***KISS?***

YOU'LL NOT SPEAK TO ME IN SUCH A WAY, **DEVIL!**
I'LL SPEAK HOW I WANT, **WITCH!**

CUT IT *OUT!* WE DON'T WANT TO ATTRACT ANY ATTENTION!
SHE STARTED IT!
CRUNCH
SNAP
STOP IT! GUYS, STOP!
WHY SHOULD WE?
SEE FOR YOURSELVES.

WELL, THESE GUYS DON'T LOOK ANYTHING LIKE SHRIMP!

YOU **COULD** HAVE **WARNED** ME, YOU KNOW.
WOW! THAT WAS SOME FALL.
WELL, I'M JUST **SO** HAPPY I COULD **ENTERTAIN** YOU, GOAT!
I COULD HAVE **DIED!**

I'M HAPPY YOU DIDN'T DIE.
THAT WOULD HAVE REALLY MESSED UP MY PLANS.
I SURE WOULD HATE TO MESS UP YOUR GOAT PLANS.
WHAT BROKE MY FALL?
THAT WOULD BE MY BODY.
YOUR WHAT?!

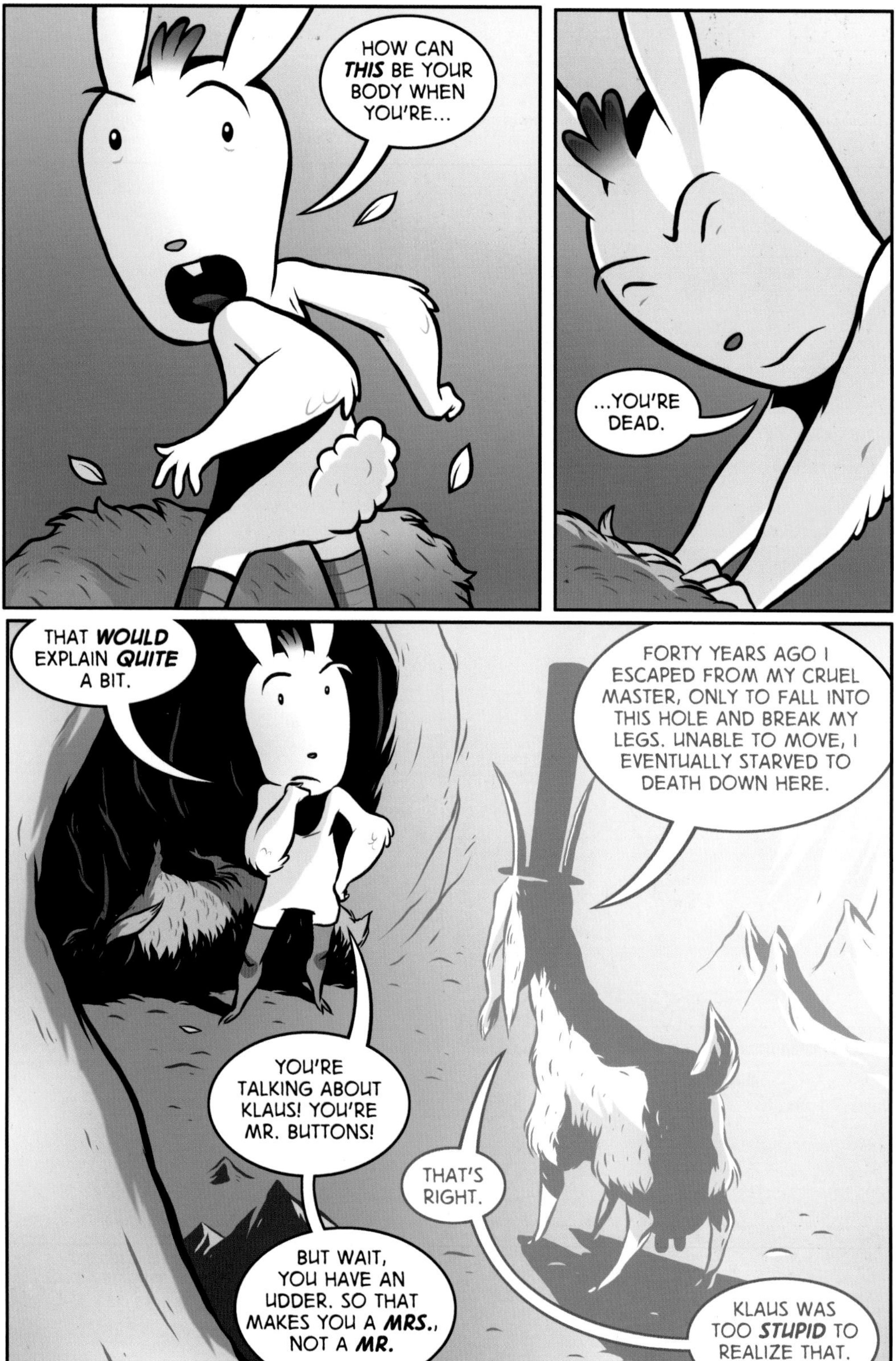
HOW CAN THIS BE YOUR BODY WHEN YOU'RE...
...YOU'RE DEAD.
THAT WOULD EXPLAIN QUITE A BIT.
FORTY YEARS AGO I ESCAPED FROM MY CRUEL MASTER, ONLY TO FALL INTO THIS HOLE AND BREAK MY LEGS. UNABLE TO MOVE, I EVENTUALLY STARVED TO DEATH DOWN HERE.
YOU'RE TALKING ABOUT KLAUS! YOU'RE MR. BUTTONS!
THAT'S RIGHT.
BUT WAIT, YOU HAVE AN UDDER. SO THAT MAKES YOU A MRS., NOT A MR.
KLAUS WAS TOO STUPID TO REALIZE THAT.

SO, IF YOU'RE DEAD, WHAT ARE YOU DOING HANGING AROUND *HERE* FOR?
UNFINISHED BUSINESS...
...AND THAT *ISN'T* A CHAIR.
OH! RIGHT! SORRY.
NO PROBLEM. COME WITH ME, I'LL EXPLAIN EVERYTHING. OH, AND BRING MY BODY.
THIS JUST KEEPS GETTING BETTER AND BETTER.

WHY EXACTLY AM I DRAGGING THIS HAIRY POPSICLE YOU CALL A BODY, AGAIN?
WE NEED TO THAW IT OUT.
WHAT THE HECK FOR?
SO IT MOVES BETTER.
WHY DOES IT NEED TO MOVE BETTER...?
...OH, MAN, YOU'RE PLANNING ON GETTING BACK IN HERE, AREN'T YOU?
THAT'S THE IDEA, YES.

WAIT, DO YOU HEAR VOICES?
NO!
BUTTONS! GET DOWN, QUICK!
WE CAN TAKE 'EM!
ARE YOU INSANE?
HE MUST BE TRACKING ABE AND THE OTHERS. I NEED TO WARN THEM.
THEY'RE IN SERIOUS DANGER.

THEY CAME THIS WAY, AND NOT TOO LONG AGO, BY THE LOOKS OF THESE TRACKS.
UNHITCH YOURSELVES, BOYS. WE'LL BE TRAVELING ON *FOOT* FROM HERE ON OUT.
YES SIR, MR. KLAUS.

THE TRACKS LEAD UP THERE, TOWARD THAT CAVE.
LET'S GET MOVING.

BUT SIR, THOSE CAVES ARE ***CRAWLING*** WITH ***SHROMPH!***

THAT'S THE WAY WE'RE GOING, FINGERBONES!
ALL OF US!

BUT SIR, I'M REALLY IN NO CONDITION FOR SPELUNKING!
AND PLUMMS OVER THERE IS IN SO MUCH PAIN FROM HIS BROKEN LEGS THAT HE KEEPS BLACKING OUT!
I DON'T WANT ANY EXCUSES, FINGERBONES. UNLESS YOU WANT ME TO PERSONALLY BREAK EVERY BONE IN YOUR BODY, YOU BETTER GET BOTH YOU AND PLUMMS MOVING!
THIS SHOULD BE GOOD.
NO DOUBT.

HURRY IT UP, FINGERBONES.
AAAGGH! MY LEGS!

IT'S LIKE CARRYING A GIGANTIC SACK OF STINKY OLD POTATOES.

IS THERE ANOTHER WAY INTO THOSE CAVES?
WHAT ABOUT MY **BODY?**
IT'S GONNA HAVE TO THAW ON THE WAY, ALL RIGHT?
WE SHOULD HURRY.
AGREED.

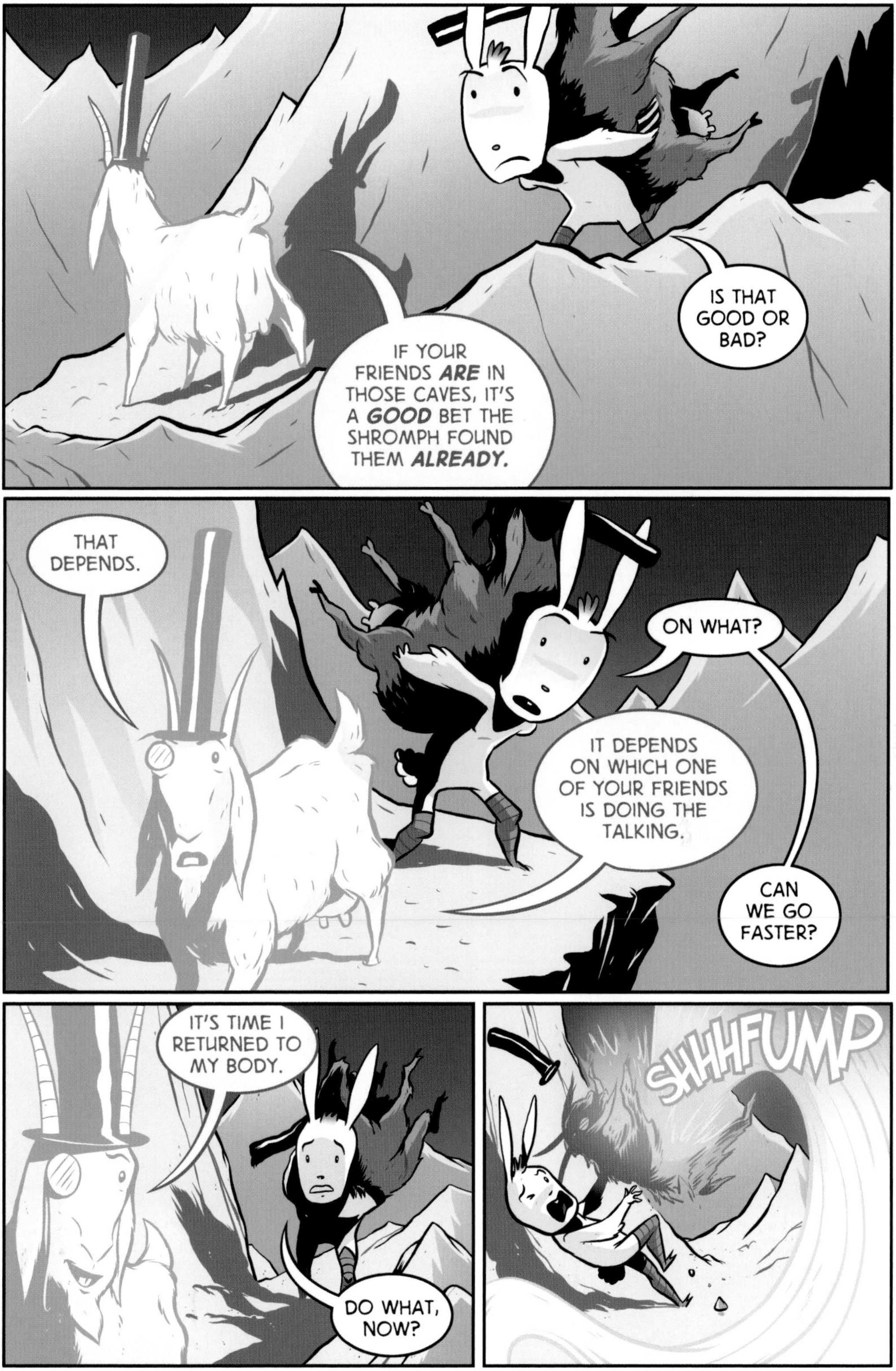
IF YOUR FRIENDS ARE IN THOSE CAVES, IT'S A GOOD BET THE SHROMPH FOUND THEM ALREADY.
IS THAT GOOD OR BAD?
THAT DEPENDS.
ON WHAT?
IT DEPENDS ON WHICH ONE OF YOUR FRIENDS IS DOING THE TALKING.
CAN WE GO FASTER?
IT'S TIME I RETURNED TO MY BODY.
DO WHAT, NOW?
SHHHFUMP

YOU JUST **COULDN'T** SHUT YOUR MOUTH, **COULD** YA?
HOW WAS I SUPPOSED TO KNOW **HE** WAS THEIR **LEADER?**
IT WAS THE **CROWN** THAT ACTUALLY GAVE IT AWAY FOR ME.

NOW, WHICH ONE OF YOU WOULD LIKE THE ***HONOR*** OF BEING THE FIRST COURSE?
PLEASE, YOUR MAJESTY, WE DIDN'T KNOW THESE CAVES BELONGED TO YOU AND --
SILENCE, FOOD!

WOW, ABE! THAT WAS **WAY** BETTER THAN I DID. **THANKS!**
YOU **MUST** LISTEN TO ME, YOUR MAJESTY!
A LIKELY STORY FROM ONE WHO WILLINGLY TRAVELS WITH A **KRAMPUS.**
YOU AND **ALL** OF YOUR PEOPLE ARE IN **TERRIBLE** DANGER!

HEY, BANJO, WHAT'S A KRAMPUS?
I THINK IT MEANS "BOSSY FEMALE."
WHAT?!
HE'S LYING, ABE! IT MEANS --
FWAP
I DIDN'T CATCH ALL OF THAT, MEG.
YOU KEEP THAT FILTHY TAIL OUT OF MY FACE OR I'LL CUT IT OFF!
I THINK SOMEONE NEEDS A NAP.

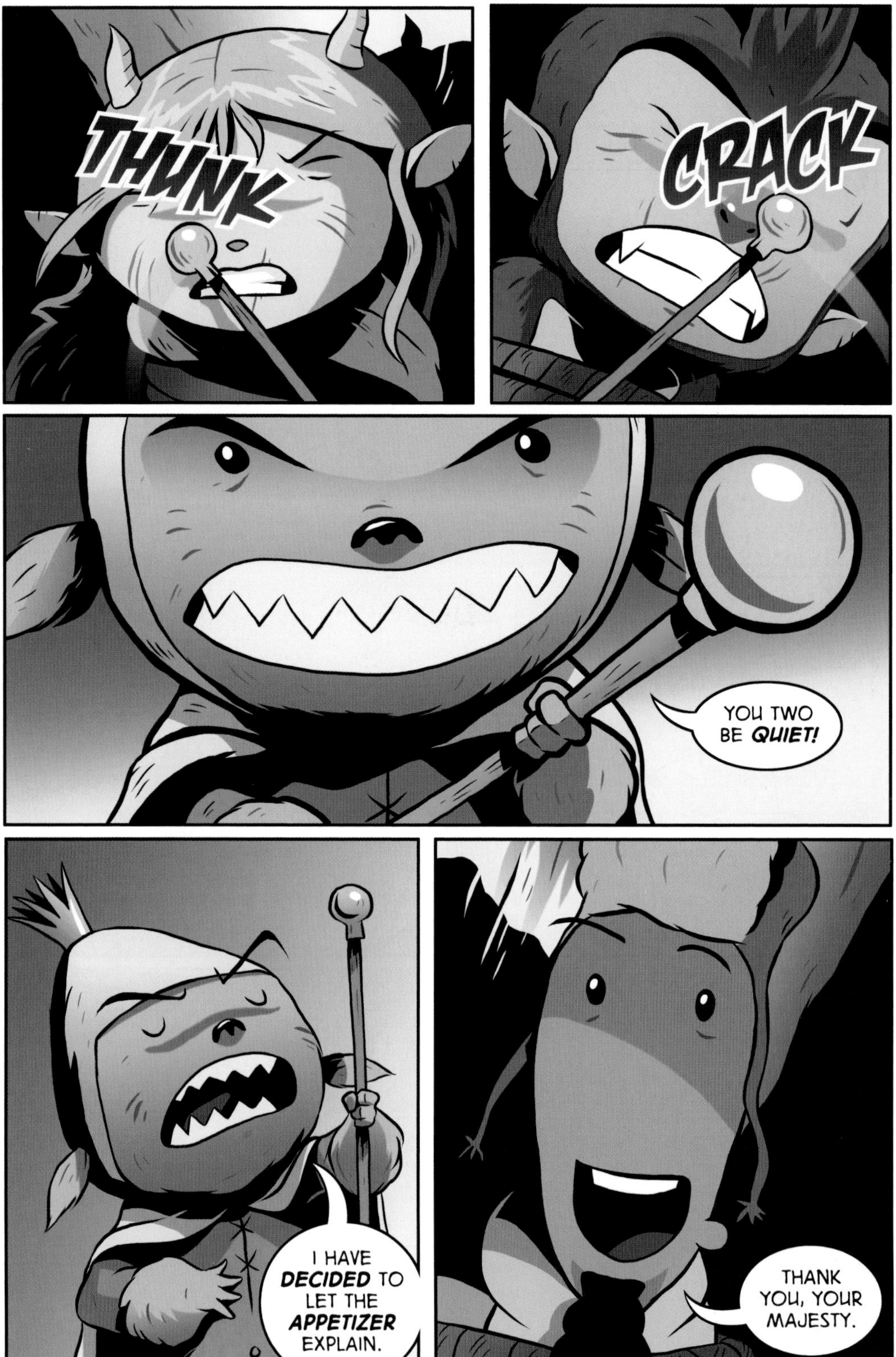
THUNK
CRACK
YOU TWO BE QUIET!
I HAVE DECIDED TO LET THE APPETIZER EXPLAIN.
THANK YOU, YOUR MAJESTY.

I WILL ALLOW YOU *TEN* WORDS.
ONLY *TEN?*
ONLY EIGHT REMAIN.
YOU *CAN'T* COUNT THOSE!
DOWN TO *FOUR.*
UM...
THREE LEFT.

"UM" COUNTS?
KEEP UP THE GOOD WORK.
YOU HAVE BUT *ONE* WORD LEFT IN WHICH TO SAVE YOU AND YOUR *DELICIOUS*-LOOKING FRIENDS.
CHOOSE *WISELY.*
THINK, ABE, *THINK!*
TAXIDERMIST!

WHAT?! WHAT ABOUT HIM?
NO!
NOT AGAIN!
IT'S TRUE, YOUR MAJESTY. KLAUS THE TAXIDERMIST IS HUNTING US, AND HE'S PROBABLY ON HIS WAY HERE RIGHT NOW!
CAPTAIN! SEND SCOUTS TO ALL ENTRANCES. IF THEY'RE TELLING THE TRUTH, WE HAVEN'T MUCH TIME.
YES, MAJESTY!

SO, WHY HAVEN'T YOU RETURNED TO YOUR BODY BEFORE NOW?
WHO SAID I HAVEN'T? THE TROUBLE IS, ALL MY LEGS ARE BROKEN, NOT TO MENTION THE FACT THAT MY BODY WAS FROZEN SOLID. KINDA MAKES IT HARD TO DO MUCH, YA KNOW?
I GUESS THAT MAKES SENSE.
AND SO YOU'VE HUNG AROUND ALL THESE YEARS JUST TO GET REVENGE ON KLAUS FOR MISTREATING YOU?
THAT'S KINDA SAD.

PUT ME DOWN FOR A MINUTE.
WHOOOPS!
OOF!
CHICKENHARE, WHAT WE'RE DOING *ISN'T* ABOUT REVENGE AT ALL. IT'S ABOUT SAVING *INNOCENT* LIVES!
IT'S ABOUT STOPPING A *MADMAN!*
KLAUS HAS BEEN KILLING POOR SOULS FOR HOME-DECOR PURPOSES HIS *ENTIRE* LIFE. WE HAVE TO STOP HIM!

IN CASE YOU HAVEN'T NOTICED, WE'RE A BIT **OUTNUMBERED**, NOT TO MENTION THE FACT THAT I'VE NEVER BEEN IN A FIGHT, AND YOU'RE **DEAD!**
HOW CAN WE POSSIBLY STOP HIM, GOAT?
YOU ASKED ME EARLIER WHY I'VE HUNG AROUND ALL THESE YEARS?
I DON'T THINK MY SPIRIT CAN REST UNTIL I STOP HIM.
IT'S MY FAULT HE HAS BECOME THE MONSTER HE IS TODAY. IF I HADN'T LEFT HIM, NONE OF THIS WOULD HAVE HAPPENED.
THIS IS CRAZY.

I JUST DON'T SEE HOW WE CAN DO THIS ALONE.
AND WE STILL NEED TO FIND MY FRIENDS.
WAIT! MY FRIENDS!
WHAT ABOUT THEM?
IF THEY'LL HELP US, MAYBE WE ACTUALLY CAN STOP KLAUS!
HOW MUCH FARTHER UNTIL WE REACH THE SHROMPH?
WE'RE NEARLY THERE.

THIS MUST BE WHERE THEY WENT IN. THERE'RE TRACKS ALL OVER THE PLACE.
LET'S PICK UP THE PACE, ***FINGERBONES!***
UGH... PLUMMS, YOU FAT ***FOOL!***

I CAN'T CARRY THIS SLAB OF MEAT ANY FARTHER!
WHAA AAAGG! THE PAIN!
THEN LEAVE HIM TO GUARD THE ENTRANCE!
DO YOU HEAR ME, PLUMMS?
NO ONE GETS OUT!
OH, THANK YOU, SIR!

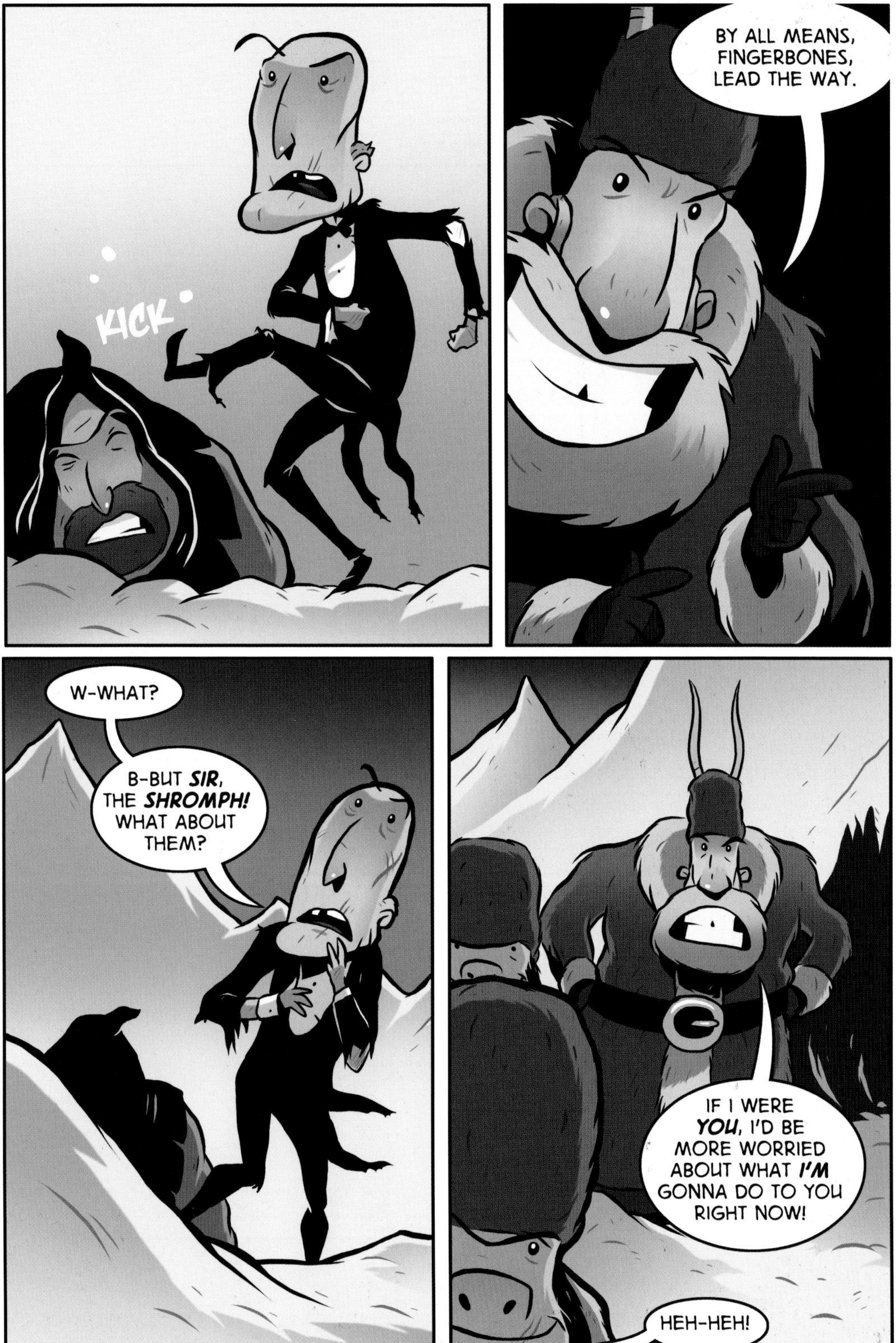
KICK
BY ALL MEANS, FINGERBONES, LEAD THE WAY.
W-WHAT?
B-BUT **SIR**, THE **SHROMPH!** WHAT ABOUT THEM?
IF I WERE **YOU**, I'D BE MORE WORRIED ABOUT WHAT **I'M** GONNA DO TO YOU RIGHT NOW!
HEH-HEH!

AND IF I REFUSE?
I'LL MOUNT YOUR HEAD ABOVE THE FIREPLACE!
I BELIEVE YOU SAID I WAS FIRST?
KEEP QUIET!
THEY'RE HERE!

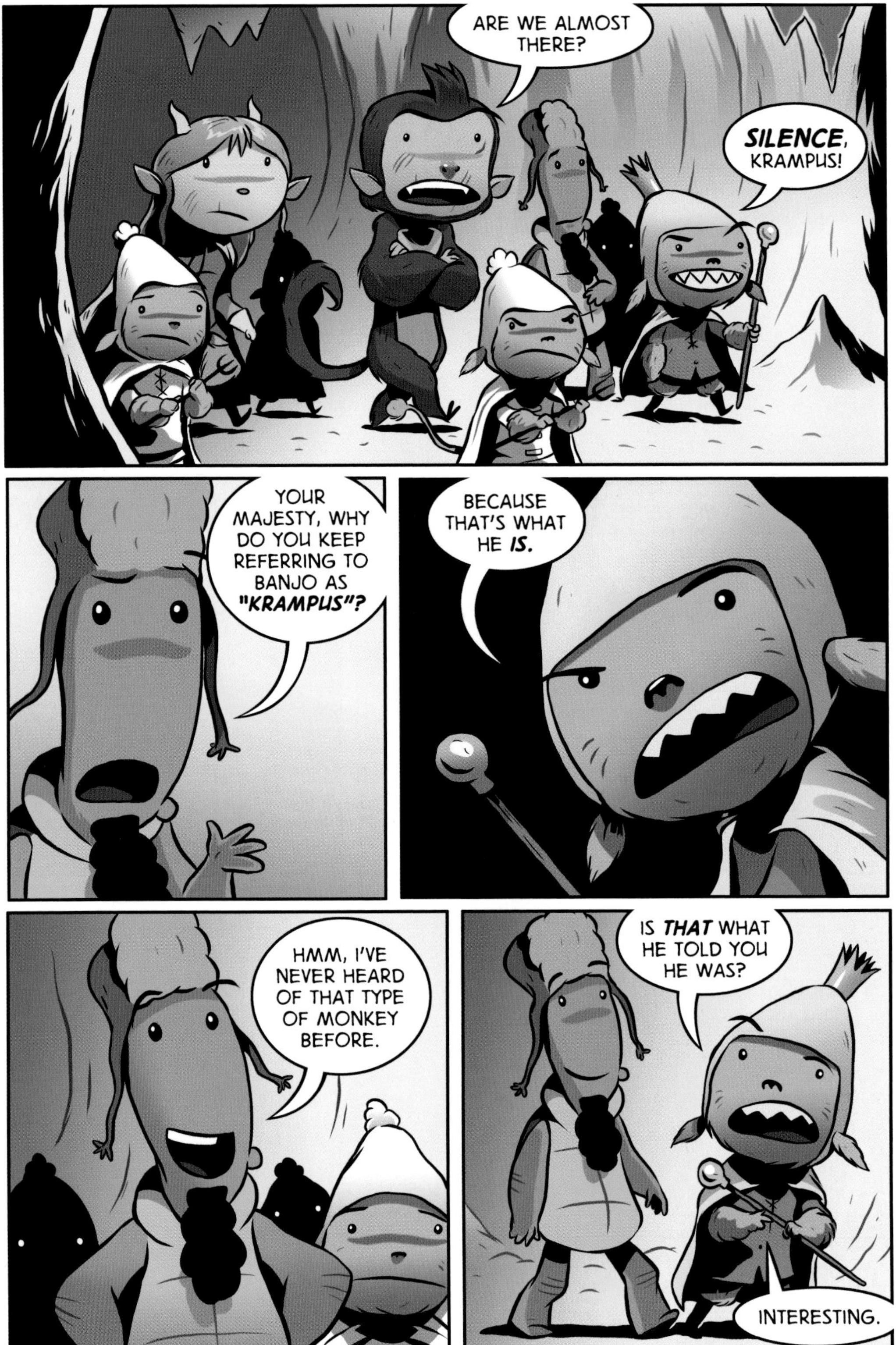
ARE WE ALMOST THERE?
SILENCE, KRAMPUS!
YOUR MAJESTY, WHY DO YOU KEEP REFERRING TO BANJO AS "KRAMPUS"?
BECAUSE THAT'S WHAT HE IS.
HMM, I'VE NEVER HEARD OF THAT TYPE OF MONKEY BEFORE.
IS THAT WHAT HE TOLD YOU HE WAS?
INTERESTING.

HEY, GUYS, WHAT'CHA WHISPERIN' ABOUT UP THERE?
THWAK
SILENCE!
WILL WE BE SAFE WHERE WE'RE GOING?
PROBABLY NOT.
GREAT.
DON'T WORRY ABOUT THE SHROMPH, TURTLE. WE'LL BE OKAY.
IT'S NOT THE SHROMPH I'M WORRIED ABOUT.

THEY SHOULD BE JUST UP AHEAD.
GOOD, BECAUSE I'M GETTING **REALLY** TIRED.
WHAT THE...?
CRICK
UH-OH! ***IT'S ICE!***
CRACK
HOLD ON TIGHT, BUTTONS!

FASTER!
I'D BE MORE THAN HAPPY TO TRADE PLACES WITH YOU!
CRACK
CRACK
THAT WAS TOO CLOSE!

THIS IS IT?
YOU JUST TOOK THE WORDS RIGHT OUT OF MY MOUTH.
WITH ALL THE TUNNELS LEADING INTO THIS ROOM, IT'S GONNA BE HARD TO DEFEND OURSELVES.
STUPID KRAMPUS.
I'M SORRY IF OUR HOME DISPLEASES YOU.

EXCUSE ME, YOUR MAJESTY! I AGREE WITH BANJO!
REALLY?
DO YOU HAVE ANY WEAPONS WE COULD USE TO DEFEND OURSELVES WITH?
I LIKE HOW YOU THINK.
WHAT DID YOU HAVE IN MIND?
ANYTHING SHARP AND POINTY!
ARE THERE ANY MORE OF THOSE SPEAR THINGIES?

OH, THOSE. WE ONLY HAVE TEN OF THEM, SO WE'LL HAVE TO SHARE.
HOW CAN THIS GET ANY WORSE?
MAJESTY! YOUR MAJESTY!
I SAW HIM! HE'S COMING!
YOU HAD TO ASK?

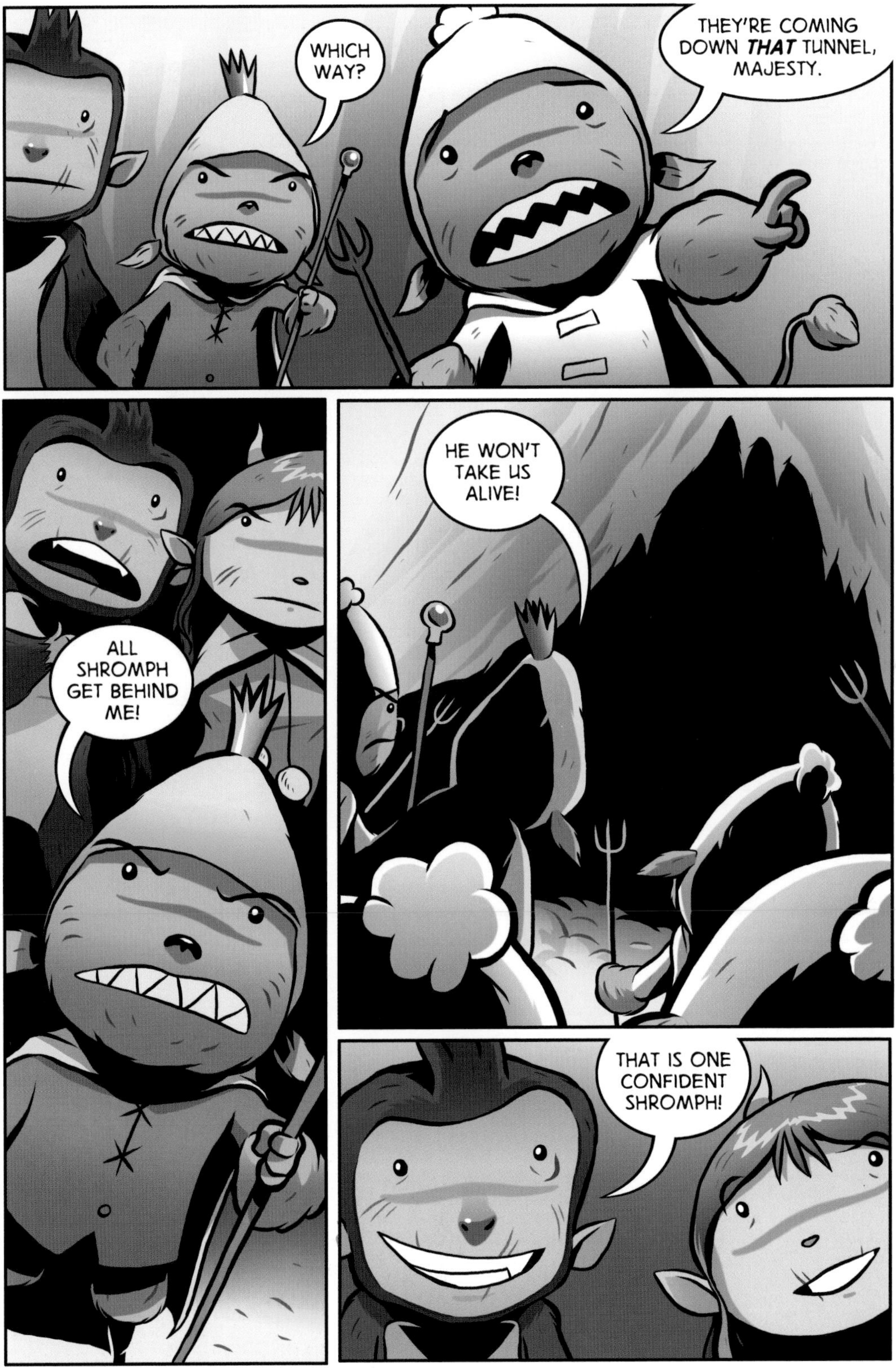
WHICH WAY?
THEY'RE COMING DOWN **THAT** TUNNEL, MAJESTY.
ALL SHROMPH GET BEHIND ME!
HE WON'T TAKE US ALIVE!
THAT IS ONE CONFIDENT SHROMPH!

STEADY, SHROMPH! HOLD YOUR GROUND!
THUNK
THUNK
TRY NOT TO GET KILLED.
THAT SOUNDS LIKE CONCERN.
NOT AT ALL.
THUNK
THUNK
THUNK
ABE! BANJO! MEG! YOU'RE ALL SAFE!

CHICKENHARE! YOU'RE ALIVE!
AND HE BROUGHT US A DEAD GOAT.
HOLD ON, HE'S WITH US.
THERE'S NO TIME! WE HAVE TO ***LEAVE*** RIGHT ***NOW!***
WE THOUGHT THE TAXIDERMIST GOT YOU.
WHAT'S WITH THE GOAT?

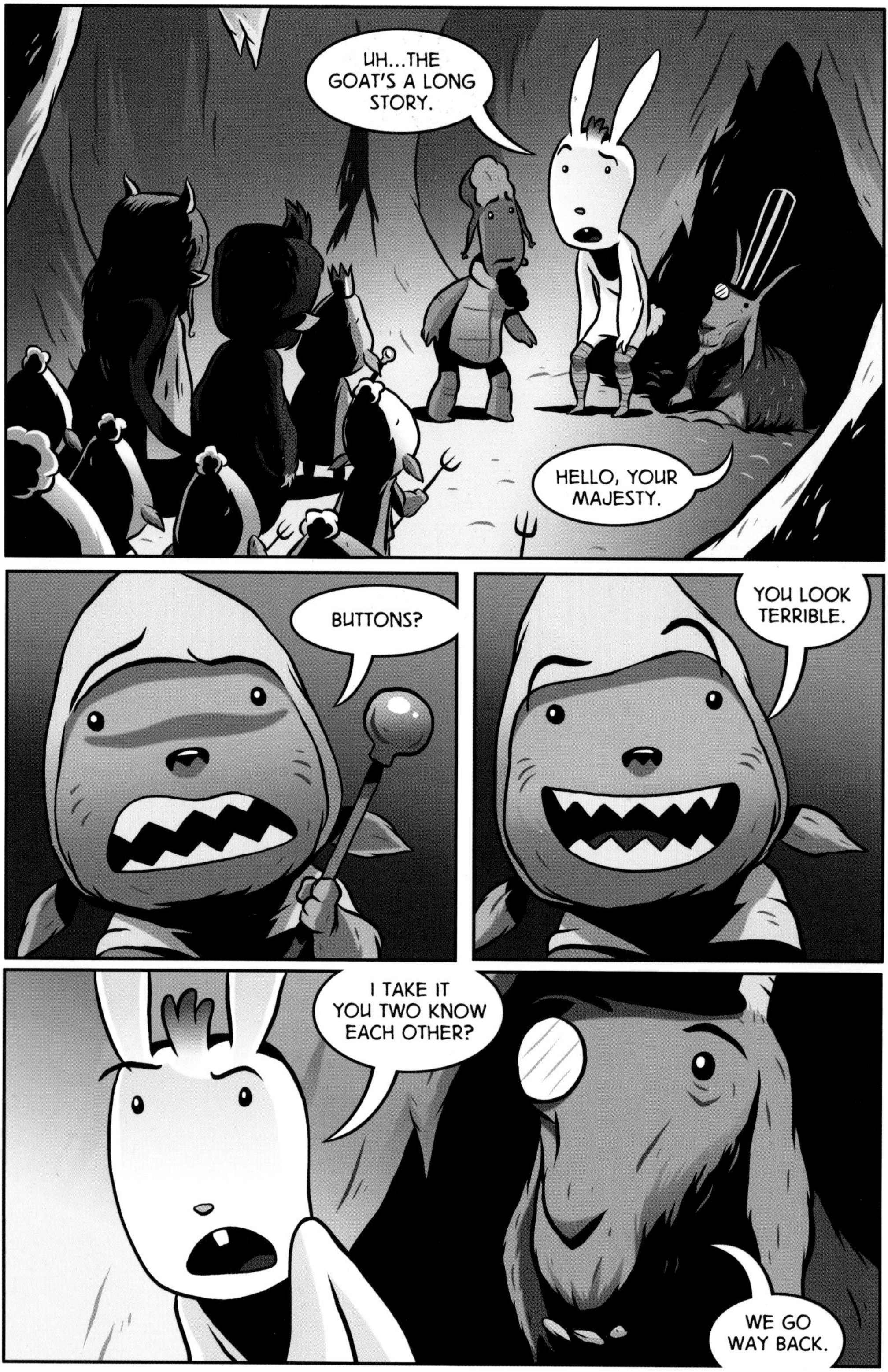
UH...THE GOAT'S A LONG STORY.
HELLO, YOUR MAJESTY.
BUTTONS?
YOU LOOK TERRIBLE.
I TAKE IT YOU TWO KNOW EACH OTHER?
WE GO WAY BACK.

SERIOUSLY, GUYS, WE NEED TO GET OUT OF HERE! THE TAXIDER...
...MIST...
YES?
WHAT ABOUT THE TAXIDERMIST?
HE'S STANDING RIGHT BEHIND YOU!

AND YOU'RE ALL INVITED BACK TO MY PLACE FOR TEA AND STUFFING!

WHO WANTS TO GO FIRST?
GET OUT OF HERE!
WHILE YOU STILL CAN!
THIS IS GONNA BE UGLY.

YOU'RE NOT WELCOME HERE, **KLAUS!**
GET OUT!
NOT WITHOUT WHAT BELONGS TO ME!
THERE'S NOTHING HERE FOR YOU, KLAUS!
THAT'S WHERE YOU'RE **MISTAKEN**, MONKEY!

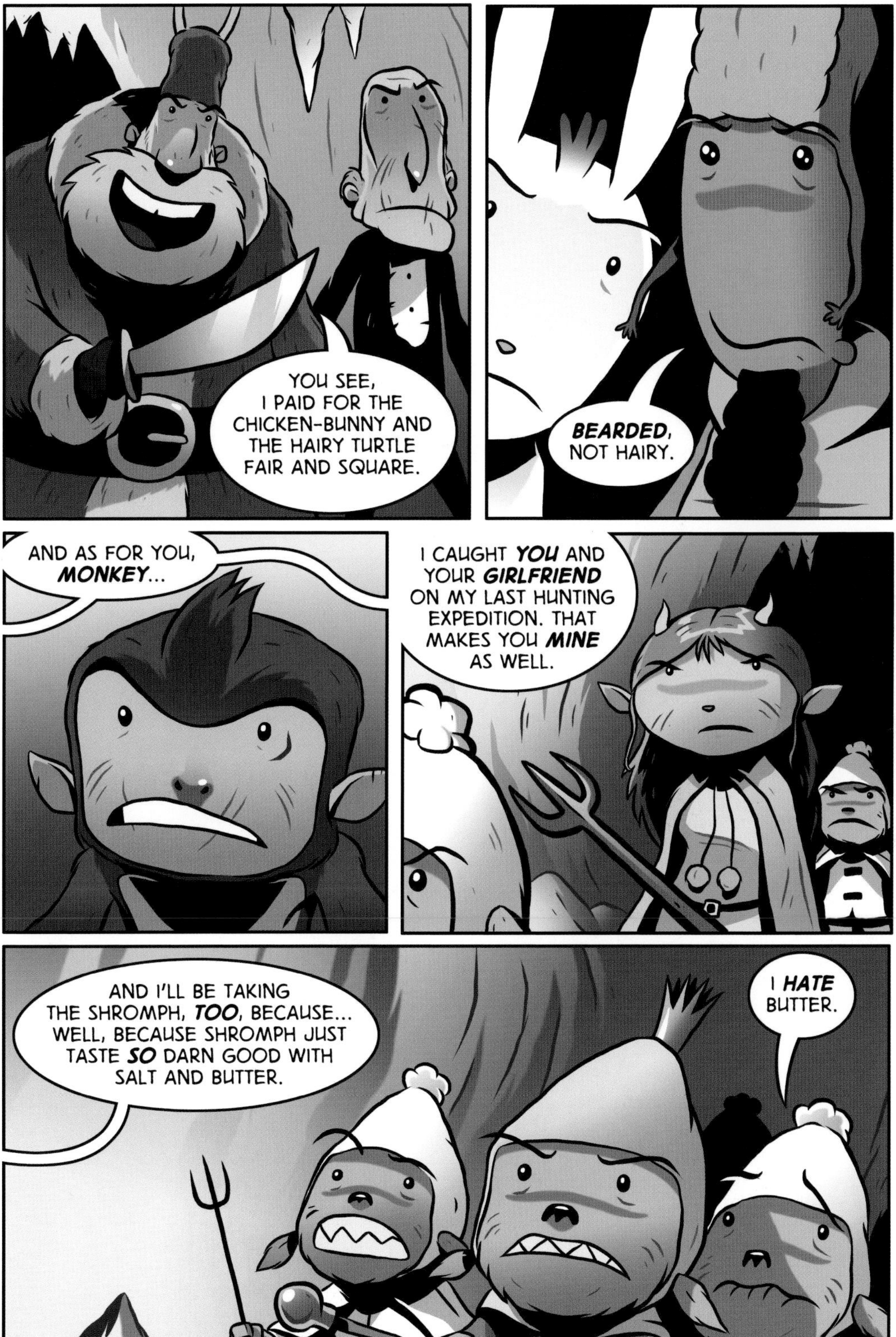
YOU SEE, I PAID FOR THE CHICKEN-BUNNY AND THE HAIRY TURTLE FAIR AND SQUARE.
BEARDED, NOT HAIRY.
AND AS FOR YOU, MONKEY...
I CAUGHT YOU AND YOUR GIRLFRIEND ON MY LAST HUNTING EXPEDITION. THAT MAKES YOU MINE AS WELL.
AND I'LL BE TAKING THE SHROMPH, TOO, BECAUSE... WELL, BECAUSE SHROMPH JUST TASTE SO DARN GOOD WITH SALT AND BUTTER.
I HATE BUTTER.

GOT ANY BIG IDEAS?
WORKING ON IT.
GO GET 'EM, BOYS!
SHROMPH! ATTACK!

I'LL TAKE THE TWINS!
GOOD, BECAUSE I WANT THE BUTLER!

KAPOW
VERMIN!

SMACK
MEG!

I'LL TAKE IT FROM HERE, THANKS!
BE MY GUEST.
I WOULD **NOT** WANT TO BE THAT **BUTLER** RIGHT NOW.

WAIT HERE! I'M GONNA HELP MY FRIENDS!
I HAVE FOUR BROKEN LEGS, REMEMBER? WHERE WOULD I GO?
YOU LIKE *THAT*, PIG-BOY?
GUH!

GET OFF ME!
OOF!

YOU ALL RIGHT, ABE?
I'M FINALLY GETTIN' THE HANG OF THIS!
LOOKIN' GOOD, MEG!
THANKS!
THEY'RE NOT SUPPOSED TO BEND THAT WAY!

I'VE HAD JUST ABOUT ENOUGH OF YOU, YOUR ROYAL HIGHNESS!
UNHAND ME, BRUTE!
MAYBE I'LL JUST UNHEAD YOU INSTEAD!
NO!

PARDON ME!
NO YOU DON'T!

I WON'T LET YOU HURT ANYONE ELSE, KLAUS!
IT'S OVER!
KA-CHUNK
AAUGH!
FASTER, PIGGY!

STUPID, BRAVE CHICKEN-BUNNY!
NO! STOP!
DID YOU *HONESTLY* THINK YOU AND YOUR FRIENDS COULD REALLY STOP ME?
DOESN'T THAT HURT?
NOT AT ALL!

WHAT?
MASTER... MASTER... STOP... PLEASE...
DO YOU WANNA BE NEXT...?
IT *CAN'T* BE!
WHY DID YOU STAB ME, MASTER? I THOUGHT YOU LOVED ME.
MR. BUTTONS! YOU'RE...YOU'RE ***ALIVE!***

WHAT HAVE I *DONE?*
I DIDN'T KNOW...
I'LL...I'LL GET YOU HELP!
PLEASE HURRY...
...SO... COLD.
CHICKENHARE, ARE YOU OKAY?
I'LL BE FINE.
WHAT NOW?
FINGERBONES! HELP, I NEED YOU!
I HAVE AN IDEA.
WAKE UP!
SLAP
BETTER LATE THAN NEVER!

WAKE UP, YOU FOOL! I NEED YOUR HELP!
...BUT I DON'T WANT TO WEAR THE RED DRESS, MOM.
SHROMPH!
I DEMAND THAT YOU HELP ME!
SOMEBODY... PLEASE.
DADDY WON'T LET YOU DIE, BUTTONS.

BUTTONS?
WHERE'D YOU GO?
HEY, KLAUS! THOSE GUYS TOOK YOUR GOAT. THEY SAID THEY WERE GONNA KILL IT!
WHAT?
THEY WENT DOWN THAT TUNNEL.
HOLD ON, BUTTONS! DADDY'S COMING!
I SURE HOPE THEY KNOW WHAT THEY'RE DOING.

FASTER! HE'S **RIGHT** BEHIND US!
WHY DID I GET **THIS** END?
IT'S JUST UP AHEAD!
ALL RIGHT, BANJO, LET'S SET 'ER DOWN... GENTLY.

LET HIM GO!
NEVER!
SHE'S OURS NOW, KLAUS!
MASTER! SAVE ME, PLEASE! THEY'RE GONNA DO AWFUL THINGS TO ME!

SAVE ME, MASTER! PLEASE!
YOU THREE BETTER GET OUTTA HERE. HE LOOKS ***REALLY ANGRY!***
ARE YOU SURE?
I'M SURE. GO.

MASTER, HELP! I'M SO SCARED!
TINK
YOU COWARDS WON'T GET FAR!
DADDY'S GOT YOU NOW, BUTTONS. EVERYTHING'S OKAY.
TINK
TINK
CRACK
WHAT?!
CRACK
TINK
CRICK

AAAUUGGHH!
CRACK
CRACK
CRACK

GUYS!
ABE, STOP!
IT'S *ICE!* STAY THERE -- WE'LL BE RIGHT OVER.
WHAT HAPPENED?
WHERE'S KLAUS?

IT'S OVER.
THE GOAT SAVED US.
HEY, YEAH! WHERE IS THAT GUY? I THINK HE ATE MY HAT.
SHE'S GONE.
SHE FELL THROUGH THE ICE, ALONG WITH KLAUS.

I'M SURE SHE DIDN'T FEEL ANYTHING, CHICKENHARE.
YEAH. SHE WAS ALREADY DEAD, REMEMBER?
THEY'RE RIGHT, CHICKENHARE.
THE ONLY THING I'M FEELING IS OVERWHELMING GRATITUDE.
I CAN'T THANK YOU GUYS ENOUGH FOR WHAT YOU'VE DONE.

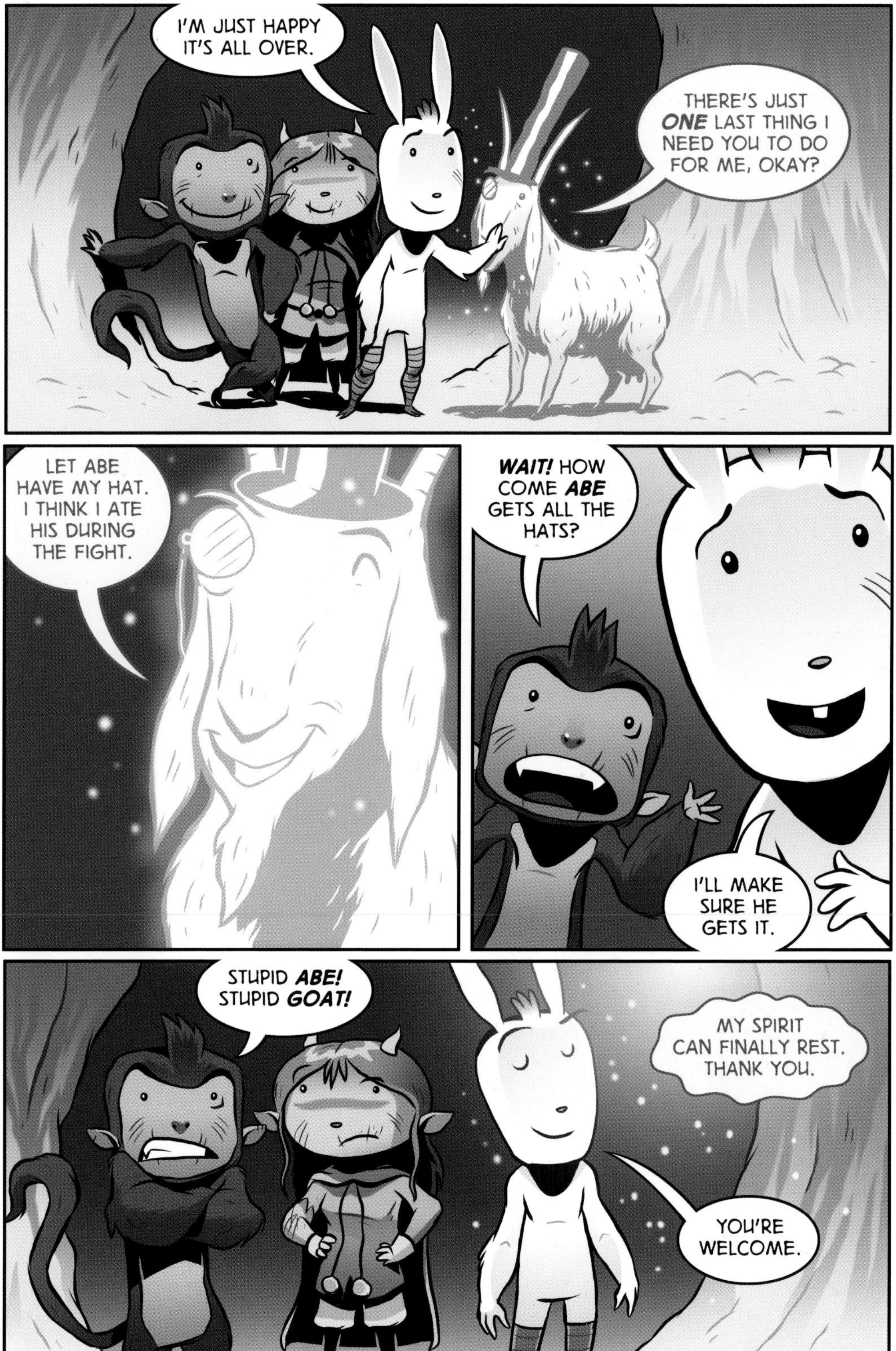
I'M JUST HAPPY IT'S ALL OVER.
THERE'S JUST **ONE** LAST THING I NEED YOU TO DO FOR ME, OKAY?
LET ABE HAVE MY HAT. I THINK I ATE HIS DURING THE FIGHT.
WAIT! HOW COME **ABE** GETS ALL THE HATS?
I'LL MAKE SURE HE GETS IT.
STUPID **ABE!** STUPID **GOAT!**
MY SPIRIT CAN FINALLY REST. THANK YOU.
YOU'RE WELCOME.

THANKS AGAIN FOR ALL THE HOSPITALITY, YOUR HIGHNESS. ESPECIALLY THE WARM CLOAKS.
DON'T FORGET THE ***HUGE*** BAG OF LEFTOVERS!
IT CERTAINLY WAS ***QUITE*** A DELICIOUS FEAST, WASN'T IT?

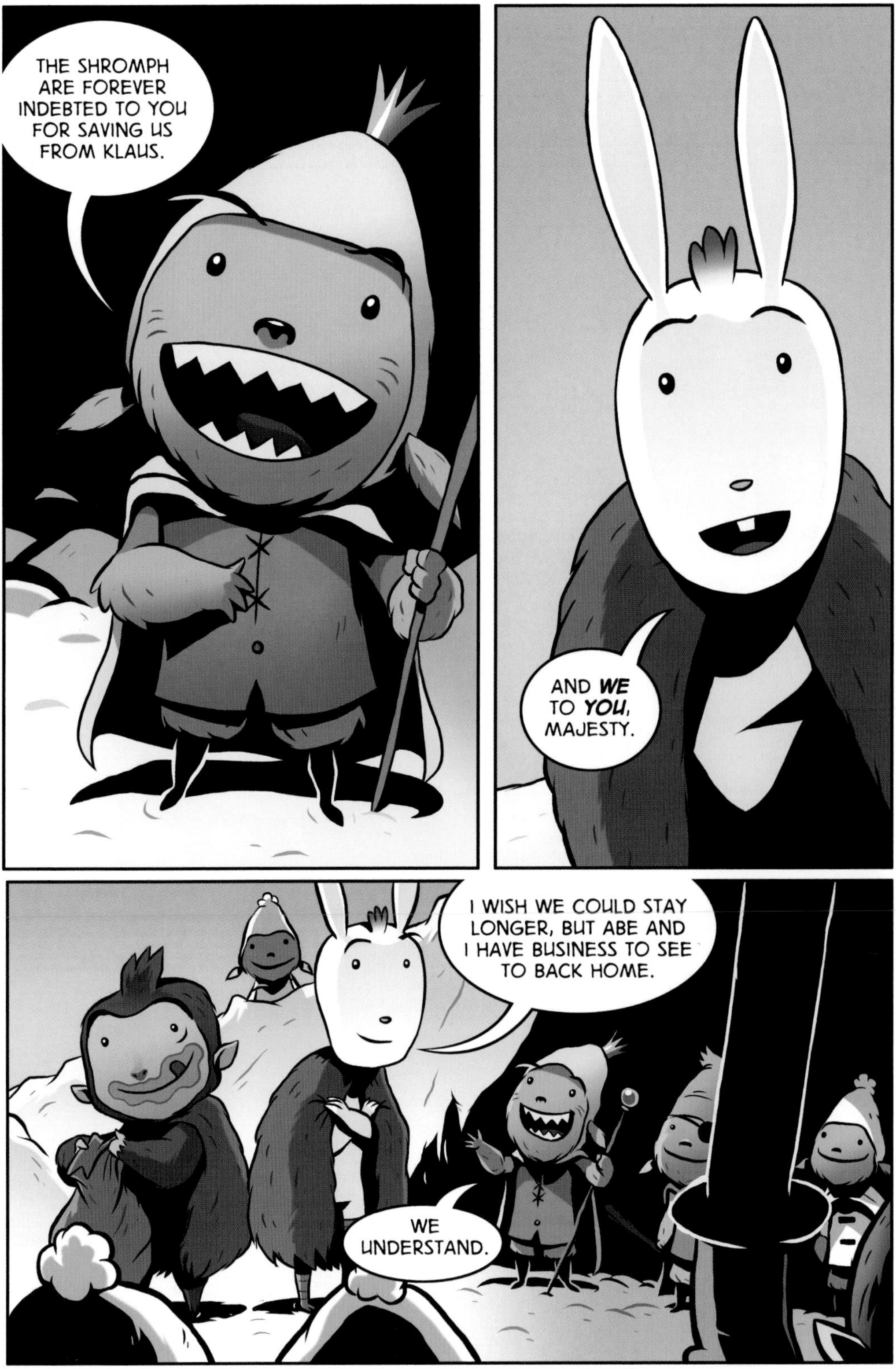
THE SHROMPH ARE FOREVER INDEBTED TO YOU FOR SAVING US FROM KLAUS.
AND **WE** TO ***YOU***, MAJESTY.
I WISH WE COULD STAY LONGER, BUT ABE AND I HAVE BUSINESS TO SEE TO BACK HOME.
WE UNDERSTAND.

MMM.
I DO HAVE ONE QUESTION, THOUGH.
WHAT HAPPENED TO THE OTHER ONES?
I'M NOT SURE I'M FOLLOWING YOU.
THE **BUTLER?** AND THE GUYS THAT LOOKED LIKE **PIGS?**
WHAT HAPPENED TO THEM?
OH, THEM!
I BELIEVE YOUR FRIEND IS FINISHING THE **LAST** OF THEM RIGHT NOW.

LIKE I SAID, IT WAS *QUITE* A FEAST!
OH WELL.

WELL, I GUESS WE SHOULD BE ON OUR WAY, HUH, ABE?
ABSOLUTELY!
UH...HEY, CHICKENHARE...
ANY CHANCE I MIGHT BE ABLE TO TAG ALONG FOR A WHILE?
SURE. IF YOU WANT TO.

AND ME, TOO?
WHY DO *YOU* WANT TO COME WITH *US?*
LET'S CALL IT ***UNFINISHED*** BUSINESS.
HEY... I THOUGHT WE WERE PAST ALL THAT?
STINKS TO BE ***YOU***, PAL!
THANKS AGAIN, MAJESTY.

I WANT YOU TO TAKE OUR ***BEST*** BOAT TO HELP YOU ON YOUR WAY.
SCABBY, HERE, IS AN AMAZING CAPTAIN. HE'LL SEE YOU HOME SAFELY.
THANKS, MAJESTY.
SHALL WE BE OFF, THEN?
THE BOAT, SHE BE HALF A DAY'S JOURNEY AWAY.

HOW MUCH FARTHER UNTIL WE GET TO THE BOAT?
'TIS NOT FAR NOW.
I STILL CAN'T BELIEVE BUTTONS WANTED *ME* TO HAVE HER HAT.
ONLY BECAUSE SHE KNEW *YOU* WOULD BE LAME ENOUGH TO ACTUALLY *WEAR* IT.
BANJO, HOLD UP A SECOND.
WHAT FOR?
LOOK! THERE'S THE SHORE.

WHAT IS IT, MEG?
YOU NEED TO TELL THEM, BANJO, OR ELSE I WILL.
WHAT DO YOU MEAN?
THEY DESERVE TO KNOW EXACTLY WHO AND WHAT YOU ARE.
LOOK, YOU'RE PUTTING THEM IN DANGER BY TAGGING ALONG.
ME? WHAT ABOUT YOU?
YOU'RE RIGHT... I NEVER REALLY CONSIDERED THAT.
COME ON, YOU TWO!

THE BOAT'S JUST UP AHEAD, GUYS.
HEY, WHO'S HUNGRY?
HOW CAN YOU ***POSSIBLY*** BE HUNGRY AFTER ALL THAT ***BUTLER*** YOU ATE EARLIER?
HOW CAN ***YOU*** WEAR A HAT THAT WAS WORN BY A ***DEAD GOAT?***
TOUCHÉ!
WHY, THANK YOU.

HOPEFULLY OUR JOURNEY HOME WILL BE FAR MORE RELAXING.
I'M SURE IT WILL BE!
THE END

CONTINUE THE ADVENTURE IN